D0456975

The
30-DAY
HEARTBREAK
CURE

			1	2	3	4
5	6	7	8	9	10	11
12	13	14	15	16	17	18
19	20	21	22	23	24	25
26	27	28	29	30		

The 30-DAY HEARTBREAK CURE

Getting Over Him and
Back Out There
One Month from Today

Catherine Hickland

Simon Spotlight Entertainment
A Division of Simon & Schuster, Inc.
1230 Avenue of the Americas
New York, NY 10020

First Simon Spotlight Entertainment hardcover
edition January 2009

For information about special discounts for bulk purchases,
please contact Simon & Schuster Special Sales at 1-800-456-6798
or business@simonandschuster.com.

Designed by Dana Sloan

Manufactured in the United States of America

10   9   8   7   6   5   4   3   2   1

Library of Congress Cataloging-in-Publication Data TK

ISBN-13: 978-1-4169-5887-1
ISBN-10:   1-4169-5887-8

For my mother, Mary
I am so proud of the woman you have become.
You are my rock, and I love you to the moon.
And of course, for the glory of God,
the Master of the Universe, who connects us all.

ACKNOWLEDGMENTS

This book you are holding has been a dream in my head and heart for eighteen years. I was not ready to write it before I truly learned it. I am ready now.

There are so many people who helped me make this Herculean dream come true. To my cherished friend and inspiration, Lindsay Harrison. Friend, you made me believe that writing this book was possible and held my hand through it all. There is no way I could have done this without you. You are my hero. When the bright shiny objects derailed me, you put me back on track.

Megan O'Brien, thank you for reaching into this magical universe and finding the best literary agent I could have hoped for. Thank you to the *other* literary agent who turned me down so that I would be free to be with exactly the right agent at exactly the right time. Which brings me to my agent, Jennifer DeChiara. Beautiful woman, this is so meant to be. I am honored to have you as my agent and my friend.

To my editor, Patrick Price, who said yes (my favorite word!) and truly made this dream a reality. Thank you for seeing my vision, for giving me your loving guidance, and for your wisdom and patience.

To the many people who have allowed me to "heartbreak bust" them and inspired me to turn it into a book.

To Michael E. Knight, for growing up with me. Our marriage may not have made it to the finish line, but our friendship is our greatest success. Proof that if you care enough, there are no failures. It's all a gift.

To Lionel Shockness, my life coach and therapist, you have been invaluable not only to my life but to this project. Thank you for helping me understand what "keeping it real" means.

To Joel and Victoria Osteen, for teaching me how to live "my best life now."

To Bill and Stephanie Loyd, my spiritual champions. You have changed me forever.

To Tony MacLaren for the magic.

To Hillary Smith, my co-star and cherished friend who took my "Officer down" call one homeless night and introduced me to Lindsay, who not only gave me shelter, but a life-long friendship. There are no coincidences. Where would I be without my best girls Anne Froelich, Gillion Shurley, and Emily Lard to name but a few. You all bless me right down to my knee-high boots.

To my sister Kim and my brother Robert, who *are* love.

I would also like to thank Frank Valentini and Brian Frons for allowing me to work in a job that I love, with people that I love being with, and with a tremendous platform for this work.

And of course, to all the boys I've loved before. Without broken hearts, there would be no lessons, no evolving, no becoming, and no book. I may not want to have lunch with you, but I am grateful.

CONTENTS

The
30-DAY
HEARTBREAK
CURE

INTRODUCTION

I Wanna Hold Your Hand

Pain is inevitable, suffering is optional.

—ANONYMOUS

The concept of a thirty-day heartbreak cure first came to me many years ago, when I was in the throes of my first bona fide, excruciating, I'll-never-be-happy-again broken heart. I had been given my walking papers quite unexpectedly, an abrupt ending to what I perceived to be a perfect romance.

The two most important words in that sentence: "perceived" and "perfect."

I instantly flung myself into every classic form of girl-loses-boy behavior. I cried my guts out. I curled up in a ball in my bed for days at a time. I stared at my TV screen—a whole different activity from *watching* TV, which usually involves some awareness of what you're looking at. Come to think of

1

it, I believe I was genuinely surprised when every news broad-cast didn't start with, "Bob didn't call Catherine again today." (His name wasn't really Bob. His name is irrelevant, and so is he. We're talking about *me* right now.) I played the same sad songs on my stereo a hundred times in a row. I didn't eat. I didn't sleep. I isolated myself. I gave my freshly painted walls and ceiling the thousand-yard stare for weeks. Ah, yes, the famous thousand-yard stare.

As my self-esteem sank lower and lower, I became more and more obsessed with my telephone. My silent telephone. So silent that I'd pick up the receiver from time to time to make sure it was working. (It was.) So silent I'd sit for hours staring at it, willing it to ring. I mean, sooner or later, he had to call, right? Even if he didn't want to *get back together*, he had to miss me at least a little and want to talk, didn't he? I felt as if my life liter-ally depended on answering the phone and hearing his voice, so I kept that phone within reach twenty-four hours a day. I even slept with it next to my pillow. Mind you, this particular heartbreak predated cell phones, so leaving the house was out of the question, no matter how hard my worried friends tried to lure me out of my self-imposed prison. They didn't matter. *I* didn't matter. Nothing mattered except the dwindling hope that *please, God*, he'd call and take a little of the pain away.

Then, one day—I'll never forget it—I quite literally *woke up* and said to myself, "I can't go on like this. This isn't me. This isn't who I am!"

And, of far more importance, it wasn't anyone I remotely wanted to be.

What happened to that joy-filled spirit I was accustomed to being? Where had she disappeared to? I looked in the mirror to see if I could find her. Staring back at me were the saddest, reddest, teariest eyes I'd ever seen and a face that seemed to have aged twenty years from the sheer weight of grief. It didn't help that I'd been too busy wallowing in self-pity and wondering what he was thinking, feeling, and doing to spend a moment to take care of myself. In other words, I looked exactly as hollow as I felt, and I didn't like it one bit.

No matter where I've lived, I've always kept a wall calendar prominently displayed to make myself focus on deadlines. I happened to glance at my calendar on that fateful morning, and then almost study it, wondering, in passing at first, what would happen if I decided to set a deadline for this excruciating pain to end?

I wondered again, not in passing this time, and the words hit me like a thunderbolt.

A deadline for this pain to end!

I've been a goal-setter all my life. I know it's important, and I know it works. What if I approached exorcising this pain the way I approached every other personal goal? What if I gave my heartbreak a deadline? What if I added "healing" to my calendar right along with "run lines with Gena" and "get roots done"? What if I set a date, made a bonded commitment to myself not to postpone or reschedule it, and assigned myself tasks along the way to stay focused on the goal of reclaiming my mental, physical, and emotional health? It was worth a try. I had nothing left to lose except my broken heart, and good riddance to that.

I took a deep breath, grabbed a red Sharpie, stepped up to the calendar, and with no thought about whether or not it was realistic because somehow I'd *make* it realistic, I wrote, thirty days from that day, the words "Heartbreak cured."

And to my surprise, the simple act of writing those words and committing myself to meaning them made me feel a tiny spark of hope. I took my first real breath in weeks. I didn't feel quite so helpless, or hopeless, anymore. I had a worthwhile project to work on and I was excited.

That night, armed with nothing but my wall calendar and my red Sharpie, I outlined the rules, exercises, and assignments for the next thirty days of my life. I made them up as I went along, keeping them simple and realistic, in a methodical progression toward my ultimate goal. I couldn't begin to grasp, or remember, feeling whole, healthy, and joyful again, but I was sure that I could handle one easy chore one day at a time for a month.

I'd scaled the highest peak of idyllic, euphoric love and then suddenly dropped a thousand stories into an abyss of deepest despair. That's how I'd been feeling. Pretty dramatic, huh? Would you expect anything less from a soap diva?

But that night, with my newly composed healing calendar by my side, I began to notice a subtle shift in my perception of how things had really gone. Those countless moments between us that I'd fallen into the habit of romanticizing weren't nearly so enchanting in the cold light of grief. Now that I thought about it without *him* at the center of every equation, I was pretty sure the sky had been a beautiful blue and the stars had sparkled gorgeously around the moon before he came along. They didn't exist just because of him, or our Perfect, Unprecedented Love. In fact, for the first time in a while, I had glimmers of awareness that I'd existed just fine, thank you, before he came along. As happens so often to so many of us, I'd simply become so lost in him and in the relationship that I'd forgotten who I was. I missed myself, and I made a promise that night to slowly but surely reunite with that nice, thoughtful, happy, funny, capable, independent woman I once was and would be again—only better.

It's one of my most deeply held beliefs that if we just stay out of the way, God, by whatever name you call your Highest Power, will drag us kicking and screaming into a better life than we could ever imagine for ourselves.

And that's exactly what has happened to me since that simple, powerful night. My commitment for those next thirty days was to nothing more than heartbreak recovery, but so much more happened than that, probably in spite of myself. With my mind and heart open to the best and healthiest I could be, I almost unintentionally found myself graced with a whole new abundance of friends, love, joy, excitement, health, work, and faith—more than I would ever have asked for and certainly more than I thought I deserved.

The same exact healing and abundance can happen for you. You're in too much pain to believe me right now, but that's okay. I believe it enough for both of us.

Relax.

Breathe.

Follow the instructions in this book, the ones that, to my amazement, worked for me.

Most of all, as the saying goes, don't think about it, just do it.

There's a second reason for my passionate determination to write this book, and it's as intensely personal as the first.

As you know, we all need a purpose in life. Even as a child I knew that mine was acting. I would be an actress, no doubt, no questions asked, no stopping me. And I have no regrets about that childhood decision. Not one. I treasure my acting career. Even on my worst days there isn't a single minute when I'm not grateful to be doing the very thing I dreamed about for as long as I can remember.

But after making a generous living at it for twenty-nine years, I began to realize that acting was only part of my true purpose. The older and wiser I got, the more I found myself wondering why on earth I'm really here, and what on earth I'm really here to do. Wondering made me dig deeper into my soul and ask some hard questions that only I could answer.

What do I love?

What would make me so happy that I would do it for free full-time if I didn't have to worry about paying my bills?

What would truly fill me up?

Thank God, the answers were swift. And simple.

I love loving.

I love people.

I love connecting.

I love speaking.

I love writing.

I love inspiring.

I love healing.

I love hugging.

I love holding your hand.

With those realizations in mind, the greater part of my purpose finally came shining through: I'm here to help you find your way back to you, reminding you, and myself, that every step of the way, we really are all in this together.

And that includes the numb, stupid, sad, angry, confused pain of heartbreak, which has a grief all its own. You've never been more aware of that fact than you are right now, or you wouldn't be reading this book and giving me this opportunity to lift some of that singular darkness.

It really is amazing how alike we all become when the darkness of heartbreak sets in. The thousand-yard stare. The inability to think, focus, sleep, or eat like a normal person. The unfortunate, almost unconscious talent for making him the sole topic of every thought and conversation. The incessant mantra of free-fall confusion that usually starts with that tricky word, "Why?" and inevitably leads to endless fantasy scenarios of woulda, coulda, shoulda, and what if? And then, when the confusion gets too monotonous, the equally inevitable blame game—either blaming him for everything wrong in the world, including static cling and global warming, or assuming all the blame for the breakup and beating ourselves to a pulp over it. The same tape seems to play in all our heads when we're heartbroken, repeating hurtful words like "loser" and "inadequate" and "fool" over and over again, a dark depressing tape we inadvertently choose to keep playing.

It took me a long time to discover that, yes, I was choosing to let that tape play, and that, yes, just as surely, I could choose to stop it. The off button exists. The hard part is finding it and then insisting on pushing it, taking responsibility for where we are, how we got here, and what we're going to do about it.

The good news is, taking responsibility is worth it.

We can't heal without it, and it's an important part of the journey we're about to take together.

But for now, right this moment, I just want to hold your hand.

You've probably learned one of the same things I have in the course of various and sundry relationships: when the end comes and the pain sets in, it's pretty much irrelevant whether he left you or you left him, or how short- or long-term the ended relationship was. It hurts, and that makes it important. While you and I spend the next thirty days together through the pages of this book, you have my word that you'll never find me trivializing your heartache no matter what the circumstances that caused it.

What I will do is keep reminding you as we go along that I understand, I care, I've been there, and guess what?

I'm still here. Safe and sound. And believe it or not, so are you.

Hello, beautiful.

I see you.

I know you.

Welcome to the beginning of the end of your heartbreak.

As you and I walk this journey together, hand in hand, for the next thirty days, I'm going to be giving you a series of assignments and exercises, in a very deliberate order, one per day and *only* one per day. There are several reasons that I'll ask you not to rush through any chapter or exercise and not to skip to the next one, no matter how tempted you might be! If you do you'll be robbing yourself of the value of that day's assignment and, in the long run, the full benefits of this carefully designed progression of healing. It's not unlike that day we've all been through when we decide we're going to get in shape. The worst mistake we can make, no matter how many times we're warned against it, is to get in too big a hurry, do more leg lifts and stomach crunches and treadmill minutes than we're ready for, and end up so stiff and sore the next day that we give up. This book isn't the *1-Day Heartbreak Cure*, after all, nor is there any such thing. It's the *30-Day Heartbreak Cure*, with each day designed to lead into the next and each day having enough value to warrant your full, undivided attention. Every time you're tempted to jump ahead, remind yourself, "Stay in the present moment. Stay in the present moment." The present moment is a safe place to be. You're okay in the present moment. You're in pain, but all is well. Hard as it is to believe, you're not dying.

And I'm here. By your side. Holding your hand. Crying

with you until we can laugh together. And we will, you have my word.

Are you ready?

Are you ready to get past your pain and move on to the great life that's waiting for you?

Are you ready to relearn the joy of taking charge of yourself again, and reclaiming the control you handed over to someone who clearly didn't deserve it?

I know you're ready.

Because you're already several pages into being on your way.

Now, take my hand and repeat after me, out loud. Yes, I'm serious, OUT LOUD:

Today I love and respect myself enough to begin the process of healing. For the next thirty days I commit myself to learning and growing and remembering how to celebrate my ability to move ahead even stronger and better than I was before. In the meantime, I'll be grateful for every tear I cry, because every tear is my grief leaving my spirit, to be replaced with love, joy, and the grace of inner peace.

DAY 1

The Rules:
Cry Yourself a River

*I never work better than when I am inspired
by anger; when I am angry, I can write, pray,
and preach well, for then my whole tem-
perament is quickened, my understanding
sharpened, and all mundane vexations and
temptations depart.*

—Dr. Martin Luther King Jr.

I t's over.

You're devastated, numb, angry, lost, hurt, helpless, hopeless, shaken—any adjective that applies to grieving applies to
you right now. Although in a way, this may be worse, because
the source of your grief has the arrogant nerve to still be alive,
probably having himself a perfectly good day, while you feel as
if you're dying inside.

You have no idea what to do or where to even start to relieve the pain, let alone fathom your life without this man who hasn't been out of your thoughts for more than five minutes at a time. Without him to take up all that mental and emotional space, without him to plan around and fantasize about and dress for and look forward to, how will you ever recognize yourself again?

Let's face it, at the core of all its most hideous qualities, heartbreak strips you of your ability to think clearly, your sense of structure and logic, and, maybe worst of all, your most basic, innate desire to take care of yourself.

I know. I've been there. More than once.

So I'm here, right beside you, holding your hand, fully prepared to do those things for you until—thirty days from now—you're strong and happy enough to be in charge again, not just back to normal but better than ever. (It's okay that you don't believe it at the moment. I believe it enough for both of us.)

And what helps bring clarity, structure, logic, and self-care to our lives more simply than rules?

Yes, there are rules for this journey of recovery we're embarking on together. I was tempted to call them "prescriptions" for those of you who think the word "rules" is a synonym for confinement. But I'm not willing to take even the slightest chance that by "prescriptions" you'll think I'm encouraging a trip to your nearest pharmacy, especially at a time when you might find that to be a temptingly attractive idea. So we'll stick with "rules," with the promise that in the end they won't be confining, they'll be downright liberating.

* * *

Your assignment for Days 1 to 3 is to simply read each day's rules and promise yourself you'll follow them every single day for the next month, for one good reason: they work! Read them once, or a hundred times. Make copies and put them everywhere you'll have easy access to them for reinforcement—in your purse, on your nightstand, in your car, on the refrigerator, anywhere and everywhere you won't be able to ignore them, no matter how much you might want to. And trust me on this, when it comes to some of these rules, you'll want to ignore them. Just don't. Period. If you're afraid you might get weak, or ornery, or too depressed to bother, give a copy to your most trusted, willing friends and ask them to help keep you on track. Look at it this way: you only have to follow these rules for thirty days. There's nothing you can't handle for thirty days, except feel like you're feeling today.

Right now, today, you're barely functioning, and your concentration level and attention span are challenged, to say the least. Anything beyond the basics is going to feel like more work than you care to handle. So let's keep it simple and straightforward. These are your no-kidding-around, no-excuses rules to read and follow from Day 1.

First, You Cry

I know. You hardly need me to suggest it, let alone give you permission. Go right ahead. Curl up in a ball and cry like you've never cried before if you want to. Save the stoic false bravado for some other time. This hurts, and it's the most normal thing in the world to cry when you're hurt.

Just one condition: you only get three days for this full-blown crying jag. Three days. That's it. So make it good.

No Isolating

Let your best, most supportive, most positive friends know what you're going through, and tell them you need them. Don't leave it to them to figure it out—very few of us are skilled at mind reading, after all.

In fact, feel free to adopt a policy my closest friends and I have borrowed from various law enforcement agencies. When one of us is in real trouble, emotional or otherwise (and false alarms are strictly prohibited), we call the best of the best with the simple words "Officer down." It's great shorthand to rally the troops, and whoever can't get there in person can send plenty of love and cheerleading by phone and e-mail.

Remember to choose your "Officer down" friends carefully. These friends always seem to know what to do in a crisis and make you feel safe, valued, and good about yourself. Assemble them instantly.

You may also have "friends" (for lack of a more appropriate word) who'll be eager to remind you that they told you a hundred times to dump this loser, that they would never have been dumb enough to fall for him in the first place, and that it's about time you woke up and smelled the coffee. You may even get a strange (accurate) feeling that they're taking a hint of delight in your misery. Avoid them like the plague, at least for now if not for the rest of the happy, healthy life you have to look forward to.

No Retail Therapy

Extreme as that sounds, especially when you're already feeling deprived enough, thank you, I promise that except for the most basic necessities, this is *not* the time to shop till you drop. You're not in the right frame of mind to pick out anything great anyway, and you're bound to eventually hate every item you drag home because it will remind you of the misery you were in when you bought it.

Besides, if you think you're an emotional wreck now, wait till you see how much worse you'll feel when you're this unhappy *and* in debt up to your shoulders.

In fact, this is an ideal time to clean out your closet, which you've been meaning to do for ages, and donate all those perfectly good but unused items to charity. Whether it was your idea or the heartbreaker's, you've already got momentum going toward eliminating useless clutter from your life, right? So why not let your closet and some truly worthy charities take the best possible advantage of that momentum?

Weight Management

Take it from a woman who's battled her weight her whole life. I've been anorexic as well as overweight, depending on the state of my emotional well-being. It's a daily challenge, but I can honestly say I feel great about myself today, and *that's all that matters.* It takes work, but I'm worth it, and so are you!

If your weight is higher than you'd like it to be, seek out a life plan—not a diet—that you can make friends with. If you're underweight or you're one of those women who lose their appetite when they're anxious or depressed, this is exactly the time to declare war on your lack of desire to eat. And war is not too strong a word. I don't just want you to throw down a mouthful or two of anything you happen to walk past. I want you to stock your refrigerator and cupboards with healthy foods you like (not the oxymoron it appears to be if you really think about it) and eat four to six small "meals" a day. Your mind will thank you, your emotional stability will thank you, your energy level will thank you, and your physical shape will thank you.

It's worth repeating what I said earlier about plunging yourself into debt: You think you're miserable now? Wait till you see how much worse you'll feel if you let your weight spin out of control one way or the other. I've been there. It's not pretty.

They say success is the best revenge. I don't disagree with that. But I would add, "So is the best body you've ever had."

There. That's enough work for today.

Reread this chapter a few times. Or curl up and have another good cry. Or soak in a hot bubble bath and then head straight to bed.

But first, draw a nice big *X* inside the initial box of the thirty-day calendar in the front of this book, and give yourself a big hug. Instead of giving in to the temptation of doing absolutely nothing but wallow in your grief, you chose to move yourself one step closer to healing. I'm proud of you, I'm pulling for you, and I'm looking forward to our time together tomorrow.

DAY 2

More Rules, More Crying

Take away the cause and the effect ceases.

—MIGUEL DE CERVANTES

Hello again, my friend. Welcome to Day 2. I'm glad to see you. And don't worry about drying your eyes on my account. I promised you three days of crying and I meant it. Go right ahead. Have at it, for as long as you want. In the meantime, let's talk about today's helping of nonnegotiable rules for the next twenty-nine days. Remember, you won't be thrilled with all of them, but you'll thank yourself later for following them to the letter, because—repeat after me—they work!

No Excesses, Ever!

Let's face it, your mind isn't functioning at its healthiest, most rational, most self-protective best right now. The obvious temptation is to indulge yourself in whatever might distract you, anesthetize you, or make you feel better if only for a few short hours. Alcohol, drugs, gambling, chat rooms on the phone or on the Internet—*anything* you know perfectly well is both potentially destructive and habit-forming. List the ones that tempt you the most, and then title the list "My Worst Enemies," because I promise, that's exactly what they are.

Easier said than done. Moments are bound to come along when your gut reaction is, "I don't care." But when the stakes are as high as they are when you're feeling an urge toward risky behavior, you have to finish the thought, and do it out loud: "I don't care *about the rest of my life.*"

And, my beautiful friend, you're much too valuable, much too worthwhile, and have far too much joy ahead to say that and mean it.

Which leads very neatly into your next nonnegotiable rule.

Be Your Own Best Friend

I don't mean that as just one of those tired platitudes we've all heard so often they've stopped having any impact.

I mean it literally and actively.

For the next thirty days, every time you have a decision to make, or you're facing a temptation of any kind, or you're fighting an impulse you know you might regret later, your assignment is to stop and ask yourself, "If my best friend were in this same situation, what advice would I give her?"

Don't just go through the motions of asking the question. Answer it with the same loving, detailed thoughtfulness you'd offer your best friend. Verbalize it in your head or out loud, or record it on paper, whatever will make the greatest impression on you.

And then, whatever that advice might be, *follow it.*

If it's loving enough, caring enough, positive enough, protective enough, well-thought-out enough, honest enough, and integrity-driven enough for your best friend, it's good enough for you, don't you think?

Do it often and it will become a habit, and what a wonderful habit to come away with from this nightmare.

Every Day, Do Something Kind for Yourself

I don't care if it's taking that bubble bath you've been meaning to make time for, or trying a new hair conditioner or facial mask, or getting a massage, or luxuriating in the nearest Jacuzzi, or tracking down an old pal who's been on your mind for a while, or cleaning out your lingerie drawer, or filling a wall with happy photos of your life that make you smile (or will soon), or planting a flower where you'll see it every day, or, or, or. The possibilities are endless, but the point is simple: it doesn't have to be earth-shattering in its significance, it just has to be a daily reminder to yourself that you're very much worth a little extra effort, and that you most certainly deserve to be treated well.

Every Day, Do Something Kind
for Someone Else

This is as essential as every other rule in this chapter. And like those kindnesses for yourself, this daily kindness for someone else doesn't have to be monumental, or time-consuming, or even something you'll tell anyone about later. Remember that closet we talked about you cleaning out? A generous charitable donation counts as one of those kindnesses. Do you have a neighbor, or a friend, or even a friend's relative who's ill or disabled or going through struggles of their own? Offer to run errands for them when you're going out anyway, or give them a ride to the doctor, or take their pet to the vet, or help them with chores around the house that are too much for them to handle. Let someone go ahead of you in line at the store who has fewer items than you do or seems to be in a bigger hurry than you are. Help someone to their car with their overweight grocery bags. Just keep your eyes and ears open and put a little thought into it. It's amazing how often opportunities to be kind present themselves when you're paying attention, and, believe me, "every day" will be no challenge at all.

And no one has to know that you're really making all of these large and small gestures much more for yourself than for them.

For one thing, who among us can't use the karma?

For another thing, it's imperative that, even if it's just for a few brief moments, you think about something besides your own misery and, even worse, *him*.

For yet another thing, you need more than usual to feel cared about right now, and the greatest success we'll ever achieve in this life is to give away what we ourselves need the most.

And finally, let's face it, it's almost impossible to get through a breakup without our self-esteem taking a nosedive. I've never found a quicker, easier, more cost-efficient way to feel better about myself than when I've extended a helping hand to someone I could have just as easily passed by.

And now, draw a nice big *X* through Day 2 on your calendar, cry some more while you've still got the chance, and rest up, because tomorrow we're going to tackle the rules you've been braced for: the rules about *him*.

DAY 3

Your Last Day of Crying and the Rules About Him

When you're busy fighting alligators, it's easy to forget you have friends on the shore.

—Pat Love

Isn't it perfect that you'll be using up your final quota of tears on this third day, the day we're going to be focusing a lot of our attention on the man who triggered them? Of course, it's precisely because today's rules will be the hardest rules to follow for the next thirty days that they'll be among the ones that will make the most difference, and that I've saved them for Day 3, when you're a little stronger than you were on Days 1 and 2.

Take a moment to notice that and applaud yourself for it—you really are a tiny bit stronger today, and good for you!

Okay. Here we go. Brace yourself, and repeat one more time the reason for these rules: they work!

No Contact

That's right. No contact with the heartbreaker for thirty days. None. Zip. Zero. Nada.

I'm begging you. And I mean it.

No calling him. Not even just to hear his voice on his answering machine. (See what I mean? I really *have* been there.) To insist on revisiting something or someone who's caused you this much pain is exactly like saying, to quote a friend of mine, "That stove won't be hot *this* time!"

No accepting calls from him. If you don't already have caller ID, it's worth the investment just to make sure you know which calls to ignore. He had all the opportunities in the world to talk to you *before* he broke your heart, and look what he did with them. Anything further he has to say is just noise, nothing more. Don't forget, it's entirely possible that he doesn't necessarily want you back, but he doesn't want you to get over him either. (And come on, we women have been known to be guilty of that game too, so let's not get too indignant about it.) You need to hear his voice, especially if he's being sweet and saying everything you've been yearning to hear him say, exactly as much as you need to tie yourself to the bumper of a bus and get dragged around town for a day or two. In the long run, it's not just possible but probable that you'll wish you'd opted for the bus.

By the way, for the record, yes, "no contact" does include his family, his friends, his coworkers, and anyone else you met through him.

There's one and only one inevitable result from contact with him during this thirty-day program you and I have embarked on together: whether that contact goes well or badly, *you're going to backslide.* You're going to spend another day down the line feeling as despondent as you feel today, and starting this book again from page one, and I know you don't want that. The one and only way to avoid it is to avoid him, no matter how hard it is.

And here's the good news: after thirty days, if you strictly adhere to the no-contact rule, you'll discover that you don't care nearly as much as you thought you would. Been there, done that; and I swear to you, you won't believe what a liberating difference it makes.

Go Right Ahead, Think About Him

As if you need to be told to do that. It's impossible *not* to think about him. So do it. Have at it.

Remember every compliment, every tender moment, every gift, every irresistible smile, every time he made you laugh, every time he took your breath away, his look, his smell, all of it, right down to the tiniest detail.

With one condition . . .

The rule is that for every positive, lovely moment you look back on, you have to maintain your grip on reality and overcome your involuntary efforts to romanticize him by remembering an equally negative, unlovely moment during the relationship: the time(s) he embarrassed you, the time(s) he was disrespectful and treated you more like an inconvenience than someone he loved, the time(s) he made you feel inadequate, the time(s) he broke promises, the time(s) he was rude to and resentful of your family and friends, the time(s) he was dismissive of your priorities when they conflicted with his, the time(s) he didn't reciprocate all the time and effort you invested in him and his interests. . . .

You can make your list more effectively than I can. The point is, never a sweet, romantic memory without countering it in equal detail with a memory that just might make you start thinking of this breakup as more of a lucky break instead.

And by the way, this romanticizing him thing is bound to include a dirty trick our minds play on us when it's over. I've never met a woman who doesn't do it. I've also never met a man who does it, which is fairly infuriating, but oh, well. I'm talking about that involuntary tendency to wonder what he's doing at that very moment, particularly if there's another woman involved or, in your daydreams, a new woman on the horizon.

We never imagine that, at that very moment, he's being his most obnoxious, moody, pouty self who couldn't admit he was wrong even when it was obvious to everyone but him, and who would rather play with his Xbox than take you out for a nice dinner. No, we always imagine that somehow, magically, the instant he walked out our door that last time, or hung up the phone from our last conversation, he suddenly "got it." That tender, loving, empathetic, patient, endearing man we were so determined to inspire him to be finally emerged, thanks to us, and at that very moment he's being utterly and completely darling, taking someone else's breath away. There are probably candles involved, and strewn rose petals, and an intimate table for two, he and whoever running toward each other in slow motion until he sweeps her into his arms and carries her into a bedroom that somehow all of a sudden overlooks the moonlit ocean, where they'll spend the rest of all eternity in a happiness greater than any other happiness the world has ever known.

I would love to tell you not to even let those images enter your mind, but you know they will and I know they will. I've never been able to stop them, so how on earth can I expect you to?

Instead, to help you through these thirty days until the images start to fade on their own—and they will!—try any or all of these simple exercises to remind yourself that these scenarios are nothing more than illusions your own mind is creating.

- Every time one of your self-produced little hyperromantic movies begins in your head, I want you to reach up with your forefinger and press a spot right between your eyebrows, where your third eye would be if you had one—a spot you're going to get in the habit of calling your eject button. It's your tape, after all. You can eject it any time you choose. Even say "Eject" out loud if it helps reinforce your power over it—just make it a habit to hit that eject button!

- When you can't resist torturing yourself a little before you hit the eject button, let every impossibly romantic scene play itself out, but add the bonus of a tiny airplane flying over the heartbreaker and his new (always) younger, prettier, smarter, more successful than you girlfriend. As he showers her with his newfound charming, witty perfection, not to mention all those elaborate gifts he never got around to buying you, note that the tiny airplane is towing a banner that reads (accurately), "Yeah, Right."

- Play those scenes right on out, in all their excruciating detail, but, since you're the sole writer/producer/director/set decorator/wardrobe mistress, don't let either of them appear for an instant without wearing one of those bulbous-nose-and-glasses disguises, and/or clown feet, and/or any of your own favorite sight gags. Remember, in your movie, you can always make sure the ultimate joke isn't on you: it's on him for being dumb enough to give you up.

- Slowly but surely, begin dressing the sets of all these scenes with some little details that personify him as only you know him—that candlelit table for two can be draped with the wet towels he invariably left on the floor beside the hamper, and the bed to which he carries her can be completely covered with Game Boys, or piles of papers from work, or greasy parts from that car he's so in love with, or IOUs from all that money he swore he'd pay you back.

In other words, you may be temporarily stuck with all those painful illusions—and they will lose their strength and clarity over the next thirty days, you have my word—but if you can create them, you can modify them to make them a little more tolerable and a lot more realistic. Promise yourself you'll give it a try. It could become one of your healthiest habits.

No Revenge!

I couldn't be more serious or more urgently sincere. You're welcome to all the fantasies of revenge you want—but they *have to* remain fantasies. It's that simple.

Cling to the wisdom of the ancient Chinese, which goes something like this: "Every time you seek revenge, be sure to dig two graves—one for your enemy and one for yourself."

Write that down. If you need to, carry it with you for those times when the revenge urge might hit you. Promise yourself that you've compromised your dignity on his behalf *for the very last time.*

No Driving Past His House or Work

Especially with gas prices being so ridiculous these days . . .

You know it's an utterly silly, sometimes torturous thing to do, but the temptation to do it anyway can be almost overwhelming. Proving once again that our sanity tends to leave us when our hearts are broken. When we have to struggle to resist doing something we know at best is just plain stupid and at worst could actually emotionally hurt us, we're definitely not in our right minds.

This is one of those times when being your own best friend can make all the difference in the world.

The conversation with yourself goes like this:

"Hi, best friend, I'm feeling an urgent need to drive past his house."

"Why would you do that?"

"I don't know. To see if he's there . . ."

"And if he is? You really want him to be able to look out the window and see you driving by?"

"Maybe he'd realize how much I miss him and come outside or something."

"Or maybe he'd think it's a little pathetic that you have nothing better to do and start wondering if he's got a potential stalker on his hands. That's endearing, isn't it? It's far more likely that you'll just end up proving to him that breaking up with you was a good idea."

And in the end, don't we really want everyone who ever broke up with us to look back on it as the worst mistake they ever made? Not once have I ever heard a man or a woman say, "They won't leave me alone, they're there every time I turn around, I can't seem to get rid of them no matter what I do. . . . God, I miss them."

As for the bright idea of driving down a side street that will give you a view of his place without giving him a view of you, that's every bit as silly. The usual excuses range from "to see if his car's there" to "to see if he has company, and if he does, to see if it's a car I recognize."

But let's cut through the rhetoric and get to the real bottom line here, which is the essence of simplicity, like it or not.

He and his life are no longer any of your business.

And here's the upside to that, which is just as simple and just as true.

You and your life are no longer any of his business either. And hallelujah for that!

Avoid His Usual Hangouts

This can be tricky, because (a) you might easily have developed preferences for the same grocery store, the same Starbucks, the same restaurants, the same local clubs, et cetera, and (b) you might honestly believe it would help your soul to "accidentally" run into him.

As for (b), no, in the long run, it really wouldn't. I don't care how good a hair day you're having or how big a smile you can fake on cue, in the bigger picture, go back and reread the "No Contact" section.

As for (a), the usual argument is, "It's a free country, I can go anywhere I want. Why should I inconvenience myself just to avoid him?"

All true.

But I happen to be a huge fan of Dr. Phil, and he sums it

up far more beautifully than I ever could: "Do you want to be right, or do you want to be happy?"

Again, it's only for thirty days. You can do it! You'll thank yourself for it, mark my words.

Last but Not Least: Every Day, Every Night, an Affirmation

As you probably know, affirmations are repeated positive messages to yourself, reinforcements of a few simple truths that really, truly work to "pull you in off the ledge" if you'll take just a moment or two every morning and night for the next thirty days to make them a habit.

Why do they work?

Because our souls know the truth when they hear it, and they resonate to it.

So the very last thing I want you to do every night, and the very first thing I want you to do every morning, is say the following, preferably out loud, *because it's the truth*:

> *I have the power to transform today's pain into tomorrow's wisdom, and I love myself enough to choose to do exactly that. There is joy waiting for me. I deserve it. And I will be healthy enough to recognize and embrace it when it comes, and know that if this is what it took to find it, it was worth all this and more.*

And now, draw a nice big *X* through the third day of your thirty-day calendar, get the rest of that crying out of your system, and sleep as best you can. Day 4 and I will be right here waiting for you when you wake up.

In the meantime, congratulations! You're doing great!

DAY 4

Keeping a Journal

All that we are is the result of what we have thought. The mind is everything. What we think, we become.

—SIDDHĀRTHA GAUTAMA

Okay. You've had your three days of crying, and we've covered the general rules for you to follow for the next thirty days (actually only twenty-seven—see what progress you're making already?). Now it's time to dry those tears because we've got some great work to do, and it's all about *you*, my friend.

It starts with a journal.

Or a diary.

Or even a workbook.

Whichever name makes it most appealing and inviting to you.

I want you to buy yourself a nice thick bound supply of blank paper. A spiral notebook will work perfectly, as will a steno pad, or a legal pad, or a gorgeous leather portfolio. Spend as much or as little as you like, just remember that whatever you buy is going to be your daily companion for the next month, so keep those words "appealing" and "inviting" in mind.

Then, I want you to title this book by using the date we started this journey together, that is, the date four days ago, followed by a hyphen, and then the date thirty days from your start date.

All set? Great. Let's get to work.

Some of you may already keep a journal. Others of you may run screaming from the very idea of it. I have a friend who kept and confided in a diary in her early teens, until her mother unearthed it from its hiding place and grounded her for the rest of all eternity. Another friend kept a journal through her college years, revisited it several years later, and was so mortified at what a shallow, histrionic nitwit she sounded like that she swore she'd never record her most private thoughts on paper ever again.

I admit it, it took me until the ripe old age of fifty to start appreciating the incredible value to be gained from devoting some time every day, whether it's two minutes or two hours, to externalizing what's really going on with me—the wishes, the dreams, the fears, the goals, the insecurities, the anger, the hurt, the confusion, the anything and everything that are occupying my mind and heart. And at the risk of sounding like a born-again journal convert, I want you to experience that same value at this important time in your life, if only for the next thirty days. If it becomes a habit in these thirty days, great. If not, you have my word that you still won't regret the exercise.

Have you noticed that life keeps getting busier and busier, to the point where we're becoming almost obsessive about multitasking? (Needless to say, I'm just talking about us women. It's been my experience that multitasking is what we'll politely call "not a guy thing," bless their hearts.) Multitasking takes great advantage of our "short-term memory muscles," and thank God for those. But our longer-term memories and a lot of our day-to-day emotional history tend to get lost in the busyness stampede, with the result that unless we do something about it, we're perpetually shortchanging the most substantial aspects of who we are, what's genuinely affecting us, and why we're feeling what we're feeling. I can memorize twenty or thirty pages of dialogue on *One Life to Live* on any given day, but don't ask me what I had for dinner two days earlier, let alone what I was happy, sad, worried, annoyed, or excited about. If I don't write it down, I'm stumped. Now, obviously, what we're all having for dinner isn't necessarily noteworthy, but what we're feeling and thinking matters very much, even if it's only as a yardstick to measure our progress, or our lost ground, in those rare, quiet, contemplative moments.

I'll also own right up to a habit I'm sure a lot of you can relate to: I spent a lot of my life not just pushing but *shoving* my feelings right down to my ankles, especially when something negative happened, when I'd been hurt, or embarrassed, or insulted, or, or, or, and I wasn't in the right situation or frame of mind to deal with it. I'm sure I thought I could make those feelings go away if I pushed them down far enough, or if I refused to acknowledge them it meant they didn't really exist. Ultimately, though, take it from one who's done it, that's exactly as realistic as believing that if we stand in front of someone and close our eyes, they can't see us. I did myself some very real emotional and physical harm through all that carefully constructed avoidance and denial, not to mention repeating a lot of unproductive behavior patterns because I was just plain "too busy" to examine what was genuinely going on in my life.

For better or worse, of course, while we're darting around like gnats focused on where we're supposed to be, what to wear, and whether or not it's a good hair day, our "hard drives," or subconscious minds, are absorbing and storing every thought, feeling, and experience of our lives. Whether we acknowledge those things or ignore them, they're all embedded, taking up space, and it's a guarantee that we *will* have to deal with them sooner or later. We have two choices: pay attention and keep our emotional business current, or throw it under the nearest couch and let it sneak up and ambush us when we least expect it. That ambush can take any number of forms: a sudden, overwhelming depression that makes no sense in the context of how our life is going at the time; bursts of anger or frustration or inertia or sadness we can't explain or control; resorting to survivor behavior that hasn't worked before and isn't likely to ever work in this lifetime; or a whole parade of physical illnesses and malfunctions because our bodies and our subconscious minds are intertwined and constantly responding to each other.

All of which is to say, I believe I used to be afraid it would hurt too much to take a good, long look at my self (deliberately two words). I've learned the hard way that it hurts too much not to. And that's where the journal comes in. Especially when I'm in pain, as I know you are now, I want to be better, to understand how I got there and how to avoid as best I can being there again. If I just examine all that in my head, I can make it vanish in favor of the first shiny object that comes along. But if it's on paper, I've "said it out loud," and it's there to examine, revisit, and, with luck and work, grow from. Dr. Phil is exactly right: we can't change what we don't acknowledge.

Which is why I'm so insistent that your first real exercise is to acknowledge everything you're feeling in your heartbroken grief so that we can set about changing it. I want you to open your journal/diary/workbook and just start writing out your sadness, your anger, your confusion, your frustration, your rejection because he left you or your guilt because you left him, your failure, your stupidity, your relief, your liberation, your deprivation, your desolation—you name it, no editing, no worrying about grammar and punctuation, just write and write and write, getting every one of those things out of your head and onto those pages, like an exorcism, a purge, an exhale, a weight being lifted. All that's required is total honesty, without judgment, explanations, or apologies. Good or bad, comforting or scary, wise or preposterous, if it's going on inside you, it matters, and it belongs on those pages. Every time you're tempted to hold back about one of those emotions, think of it as a huge, lurking shadow in the corner of your bedroom. Keep the lights turned off and your imagination is bound to turn that shadow into a hideous monster, crouched to pounce on you the moment your back is turned. Turn the lights on and chances are that shadow is nothing but a harmless pile of clothes on a chair.

An important reminder throughout this first day's exercise: don't believe for one second that you're stuck with how unattractive, vulnerable, or downright exposed you might find yourself looking on paper. Feelings aren't facts, and you're going to change and evolve as you continue to grow in these critical thirty days, and for the rest of your life. This important venting you're doing is nothing but a future yardstick, I promise. It's not a brick wall.

I want you to write, write, and keep on writing for as long as you want, but no less than fifteen minutes.

Why fifteen minutes?

Because you're only halfway through with today's exercise.

The other half is entitled "(Heartbreaker's Name Here) Time."

Yes, added right on to everything you've just written, with that title inserted if you want, will be anything and everything you have to say about *him* right now. How you're feeling about him. What you miss most about him. What you miss least about him. The sweetest thing he ever said to you. The most insulting thing he ever said to you. The first time you saw him. What made you choose him to invest in. Who you thought he was. Who he turned out to be. You name it, if it's about him, no editing, nothing off-limits, write it down.

Write for as long as you want, also for a minimum of fifteen minutes.

Take note of the fact that in today's exercise, you came first. As it should be. As it probably wasn't often enough, let's face it. And chances are that once you've really let go about yourself on paper for at least fifteen minutes, by the time it's his turn some of your enthusiasm might be wearing off, your hand might be starting to cramp, and your mind might be starting to wander. To which I say *good*, and *keep writing*! It's the first step toward getting tired of thinking about him, and just think how great that's going to feel.

Today's two-part exercise is a daily assignment, with more to be added as we go along. But remember, it's *you*, your thoughts and feelings and fears and dreams and dreads, *first*, for no less than fifteen minutes a day; then him, whatever's on your mind, no holds barred, also for no less than fifteen minutes a day, even if (or *especially* if) you have to force yourself.

For now, though, as soon as you're done writing, I want you to close your new journal/diary/workbook and set it aside, take a few deep breaths, and say today's affirmation out loud:

I made it through another day safe, sound, and a little better than yesterday. Thanks to my own efforts, I even learned some valuable things about myself, whether I'm aware of it yet or not. I can't wait to learn more, and to fill these pages with increasing wisdom and the joy that lies ahead.

Now, draw that nice big *X* through Day 4 on your calendar. You've earned it, and I'm proud of you.

DAY 5

Being Your Own
Best Friend

*The wise don't expect to find life worth living,
they make it that way.*

—Anonymous

One day, more than a couple of decades ago, I finally summoned the courage to leave my marriage to David Hasselhoff. On paper it should have been one of the happiest days of my life. I was freeing myself, and David, from a relationship that had become turbulent, frightening, and destructive, giving us both the opportunity to move on to healthier, brighter futures.

Instead, I was so broken and so paralyzed with grief that I shut myself inside my house, curled up in a fetal position, and cried myself sick. I was anxious. I was worried. I was afraid. My self-esteem was so battered it no longer existed, allowing me to convince myself that I was a horrible person for leaving.

A proclamation from many of David's friends, some of whom I'd mistakenly thought were my friends too until I left him, kept echoing in my head: "No one will ever love you like that again." Looking back, the obvious response to that would be "Thank God," because it was a sick kind of love, if it was love at all by then. But at the time I heard it as a prediction that I would pay for the pain I was causing by spending the rest of my life alone and unloved, and I was sure that's exactly what I deserved.

And let me take a moment to emphasize something: I'm not assigning any blame here. I was in that marriage because I chose to be. There was no gun to my head. It was my decision to marry David, and I take full responsibility for it, and for my share of the disaster it became. I can even analyze how and why I leapt into that surefire failure. I grew up surrounded by chaos and dysfunction, and I'd simply re-created it. Whether I re-created it because I'd learned to define it as "normal" and "what love looks like" or because I wanted to overcome it once and for all I'm not sure. Nor am I sure it matters. Ultimately, I learned, I grew, and slowly but surely I figured out that peace is an option too, and I'll never settle for anything less again.

But meanwhile, back in the throes of my post-marriage agony, I isolated myself in my little room in my little house for so long that my answering machine tape ran out, full of messages I was too lost to listen to. I remember being obsessed with wondering how in the world I was going to take care of myself. It never entered my mind that I'd been taking care of myself the whole time—I just wasn't giving myself credit for it.

About eighty thousand of those unreturned calls on my answering machine were from my best friend, Cindy, who showed up at my door after a few days of being ignored. Deeply worried about me, and with a heart full of love, she was there to help me and comfort me and make me eat, sleep, and shower no matter how much I insisted I didn't need her. Talk about denial—I never needed her more. She knew it and stayed, and she made more of a difference than she could have imagined.

She opened my eyes, gently and with kindness, to some hard truths about my marriage, how I'd lost myself in it and how proud—not ashamed—I deserved to be for finally saying, "No more!" and walking away.

She loved me as only a best friend can, with no sickness, fear, or agenda, just an uncompromising, unedited, loyal heart.

Protective as a lioness, she planted herself between me and that harsh, judgmental, weak, belittling woman I'd isolated myself with for days on end—me, in other words—and chased that woman away. "To belittle is to *be little*," Cindy reminded me, and I knew she was right. I would never be as insulting to another human being as I'd been to myself in those dark days. She reconnected me with the courageous, strong, tender, loving, worthy-to-be-loved soul inside me that I'd allowed to be drowned out by years of unhealthy, negative programming.

And make no mistake about it, those voices that erode and destroy our self-esteem are an absolute form of programming. Therapists call them tapes and we play them over and over in our heads. I like to refer to them collectively as The Liar, because anything or anyone who makes us forget, even for a moment, that each one of us is a uniquely beautiful work of art is just plain lying. In fact, I happen to believe that to demean ourselves, or allow ourselves to be demeaned, translates to demeaning a cherished child of God, and who is anyone to do such a thing?

When people talk to us, they're contributing to our programming tapes, for better or worse, whether they're aware of it or not. That's why we need to be so careful about how those around us talk to us and learn to avoid those who encourage The Liar to speak up.

The good news is, if we'll just get in the habit, we can learn to turn down the volume on The Liar and insist on receiving, and reinforcing, nothing but positive programming. Our true friends, with their beautiful belief in us and their honest loving input, are reliable sources of positive, healthy programming. And by following our friends' example, we can become our own source of positive, healthy programming as well. Never doubt that words matter, whether they're someone else's or our own.

Which lies at the core of learning to be your own best friend, especially while your heart is broken and The Liar is undoubtedly having a high old time in your head, telling you what a hopeless, foolish loser you are. I know just exactly how relentless that voice can be, and how convincing, too. I bought into those lies time and time again, until best friends like Cindy and a lot of thought and study about psychological programming inspired me to learn a whole new skill that I promise can help heal your heart and change your life as much as it changed mine.

The skill sounds simple: Treat yourself exactly as you and your best friend treat each other. In other words, be your own best friend.

Take it from me, it's harder than it sounds, because it means breaking the lifelong habit of wondering if The Liar might be right after all. I'm still working on it all these years later. But it's immeasurably worth the effort. The payoff is that twenty-four hours a day the most persuasive tape in your head will be the voice of your best friend. Your biggest fan. Your fairest, most constructive critic. Your greatest defender and protector, who has your back no matter what. Your most trustworthy adviser. Your most flattering mirror. Keeper of the flame at your God center when you've lost your way. Your best friend—*you.*

Today's Exercise

It's time to get out your new journal/diary/workbook and open it to the first blank page you come to.

Now, starting today, and continuing every day for the rest of our days together, I want you to write down every self-directed insult, every negative thought, and every potentially harmful impulse that enters your mind. Yes, I mean all of them: the ordinary everyday ones ("I'm such an idiot," for example, and "I'm fat," and "You know how clumsy I am"); the heartbreak-induced ones ("I obviously wasn't enough for him," and "I'm hopeless at relationships," and "I'll never attract anything but losers"); and those ill-conceived whims The Liar can convince us are good ideas as long as we're careful not to think them through (eating your way through the nearest bakery; slashing your heartbreaker's tires; making up some lame excuse to call him, a call from which no good can come).

As you diligently write down each and every bit of negative programming you're inflicting on yourself, be sure to leave spaces between them, for a reason I'll explain in a moment. And while you're at it, stop to notice the sheer volume of negativity and self-destructive impulses that clutter your head in the course of a day.

Then, when you have quiet time to focus on this ongoing list, even if it's just a few minutes here and there, I want you to look at the entries one by one and, in the space you've left beneath them, write exactly what you would say to your most cherished friend if you heard them express that same thought. Be serious and honest about it. For example, don't write "Great idea!" as a response to "I really want to drive past his house," just to give yourself permission to indulge in a rule-breaking urge. (Remember, review the rules described in the first three days as often as you need to.) You would never encourage your best friend to waste her time and gas like that, so for this exercise you can't encourage yourself to do it either. You would never, without putting up a good fight, let your best friend demean herself, or insult herself, or set herself up for failure, so for the next thirty days—all on paper so it will make a real impact on you—you won't let yourself either. Again, nothing but the best love, the best support, the best advice, the best of everything for your best friend, and you're simply going to make it your business, until it becomes a habit, that your best friend happens to be you.

And now, take a few deep breaths, light a candle if possible, and share this affirmation with me:

Today, I make a commitment to be my own best friend. I am worth loving, and that starts with loving myself. I will be gentle and kind to myself in all regards, in words and deeds. I'm grateful for the lessons I'm learning through this heartache that will make me stronger, more compassionate toward others, and, finally, the same loyal, supportive, cherished friend to myself that I strive to be for everyone else I love.

DAY 6

Manifesting Your Beautiful Life

Don't let other people tell you what you want.

—Pat Riley

My name is Catherine, and I'm a recovering sleepwalker. I'm not talking about walking in my sleep through an occasional night here and there. I'm talking about sleepwalking through my life for a very long time, until I got it through my head and heart that the universal laws and truths of a skill called "manifesting" aren't trendy, superficial doublespeak, they're just plain fact. There really is extraordinary power in our thoughts, words, and minds. We really do attract what we put out there, and we really do make choices and construct our lives based on what we say, believe, and reinforce about ourselves.

As I said, now that I understand the importance of manifesting and have embraced it as an essential routine, I'm done sleepwalking. I'm wide awake. And on this sixth day of your thirty-day heartbreak recovery, we're going to wake you up too. We're going to work on transforming you and the patterns that aren't serving you well. We're going to work on turning your dreams into realities. We're going to help you reclaim and own your power, and treasure it so much that you'll never hand it over to anyone else again.

All that, thanks to manifesting.

And here's how easy it is: I know now that I started manifesting when I was a child, before I had the slightest idea that it was important, let alone what it was called.

At the heart of manifesting is the fact that whatever and whoever happens to us in our lives, good and bad, happy and sad, happens because *we said so!* We create the directions and events in our lives based on what we say, believe, fear, and picture, or manifest, for ourselves. We create every high, every low, every smile, every laugh, every tear. And yes, we most certainly create every heartbreak. That's not to say the heartbreaker is blameless or that we deserved whatever darkness they put us through. It's simply to say that before we met him, we somehow managed to manifest him and, as a result, reeled that mess in and then found ourselves trying to convince ourselves that it was worth the effort because, after all, we can make *anything* work. Hear us roar.

(I'm suddenly reminded of one of my favorite quotes from Dr. Phil, who's a major hero of mine: "The only thing worse than staying in a bad relationship for a year is staying in a bad relationship for a year and one day." Why do we women so often cling to something that's not fulfilling us and then grieve when he dumps us?)

But I digress.

Manifesting simply means forming a mental image. The dictionary definition reads "to make clear or evident; show plainly." I've never forgotten an analogy from a wonderful book called *Creative Visualization*, by Shakti Gawain, that applies beautifully to manifesting. Going through life without manifesting is like a submarine randomly firing off torpedoes without bothering to even glance through the periscope. What on earth are the odds of hitting your target if you haven't seen it and taken aim at it? Manifesting— especially positive manifesting—is visualizing your targets and goals and not firing until you've got them clearly in your sights.

Here are a couple of illustrations from my life to illustrate the point.

I didn't just decide when I was a child that I was going to be an actress; I decided I was going to be a *soap opera* actress. Not a movie actress. Oh, no, no. Not me. I watched soaps on my nana's knee, and I remember very clearly thinking, "I want to do that when I grow up." I saw myself on that daytime TV screen with every bit as much clarity as I saw Robin Strasser and Jeanne Cooper and all my other soap opera heroines of that era. So while friends with whom I started out in show business were busy becoming movie stars—Michelle Pfeiffer, Ray Liotta, and George Clooney, to name just a few—I dug in and, guided by my childhood manifesting, began what would become a twenty-six-year career in daytime television (with a few years off here and there for bad behavior), with lead roles in six separate soap operas.

I also manifested my dreams when I was in my thirties and decided I wanted to study singing and go on to star in a Broadway musical. I'd hit a wildly precarious time in my career and, having nothing else to do, I went to see the Broadway production of *Phantom of the Opera*. It's an understatement to say that it turned me on. But just as I'd had no one around as a child to tell me I couldn't be a soap opera star, I had plenty of people, including my own agent, telling me that there was no way I was going to make it onto a Broadway stage as a singer, and that I should stop wasting my time on this nonsense and focus my energies on something realistic.

As luck would have it, my manifesting was stronger than theirs. I couldn't and wouldn't stop focusing on the image of myself on one of those vast, magical stages, singing my heart out. I was willing to do the work it took to earn it, and I loved the perpetually excited feeling of hammering away at that dream I believed in with all my heart and soul. I saw it for myself every single day. I was so intent on manifesting this desire into reality that, when I heard that the brilliant musical *Les Misérables* was casting in New York, I taped a picture of its producer, Richard Jay-Alexander, to the inside of my front door. Every morning as I left the apartment, I kid you not, I would say to his photo, "Richard, you don't know why, but you can't stop thinking about me. You *are* going to hire me for this show!" And my friends and family and agent kept on shaking their heads sadly, wishing there were some way to stop me from so obviously setting myself up for a crushing disappointment.

Two years later I starred as Fantine in the Broadway production of *Les Misérables*, hired by none other than the great Richard Jay-Alexander.

There. Now. Aren't those lovely examples of positive manifesting? Not a day goes by when I don't thank God for blessings like those.

But fair is fair, and I can't be the good friend to you I want to be without sharing an equal number of examples of negative manifesting from my life. And I need to add that manifesting doesn't always include literal mental images. Thoughts and concepts typically form pictures of some kind in our minds, so they count too.

My childhood was virtually a nonstop parade of everything I didn't want when I was old enough to escape the yelling, screaming, hitting, alcoholism, and emotional dysfunction. I didn't see enough normalcy and healthy, nurturing, empowering love to even form images of what I wanted in the way of relationships and friendships. So the "don't wants" were my silent, impassioned mantra:

"I don't want to be with a man who talks down to me."

"I don't want to be with an addict."

"I don't want to be with a man who is emotionally abusive."

"I don't want to be with a man who doesn't respect me."

"I don't want to be with a man who yells at me."

When I wasn't witnessing examples of what I didn't want before my very eyes, I was manifesting that list in my mind, almost to the point of obsession.

That list of negatives.

Negative manifesting.

And guess what I ended up with, not once but several times—every single item on that list!

You might want to pause and review the earlier references to sleepwalking through my life, because believe me, as I was seeing to it that I completed that list and being pretty darned thorough about it, the truth never occurred to me that I had no one but myself to thank. I couldn't have been more deliberate about it if I'd advertised for every one of those don't-wants in a personal ad.

And I didn't limit my negative manifesting to relationships, either.

There was the negative career manifesting: "That other actress has more credits than I do—they'll probably cast her."

There was the negative manifesting about my wild weight swings: "I've been such a good girl, I think I'll celebrate by eating this whole cake," or, "I feel awful and I'm fat anyway, so I might as well eat this whole cake."

There was the negative manifesting about being surrounded by vast numbers of friends, without the selectivity essential to finding good, true friends, friends who'll be there whether I'm rich or poor, a soap actress or unemployed, Mrs. Celebrity or single.

Looking back, it shouldn't have surprised me in the least when a negatively manifested "friend" broke my heart far more completely and painfully than any husband or boyfriend ever could.

What we seem to forget when we indulge in the habit of negative manifesting—and I do mean "we" and I do mean "habit"—is a universal truth we should probably have posted all over our homes:

What we fear, we create.

Obviously, I've proved that in my life, and I know that when you think about it you'll find that you've proved it in yours too. We even see it proved all around us and somehow miss the point: the guy, for example, who's so afraid of his woman leaving him that he cuts her off from her friends and family, calls her fifty times a day to make sure he knows where she is, monitors her phone and e-mail activity, and so forth, until, what do you know, when she's finally had all she can take she escapes the first chance she gets. Or the woman who's so determined not to lose her man to another woman that she makes it her business to search his wallet, pockets, cell phone, glove compartment, and dresser drawers the minute his back is turned, grill him about every move he makes, pitch a fit over every woman he speaks to even in passing, and ultimately inspires him to run screaming from someone who's started to feel less like a girlfriend/wife and more like a parent/warden.

And there are more subtle, insidious forms of negative manifesting that are all too common when we're heartbroken:

"I'm never going to get over him."

"Relationships never work out for me."

"It's just my luck."

"My boyfriends never treat me as well as I treat them."

"I'll never have a boyfriend who's not (unfaithful, lazy, selfish, a pouter, etc.)."

"I'll never be as (attractive, bright, successful, funny, self-confident) as the woman he's probably with now."

All that negative manifesting, over and over again, basically programming ourselves to be losers, and then we wonder why our lives seem to run so far off track? Which, of course, is a vicious cycle—we program ourselves to fail, we fail, and then we say, "See? You see how nothing ever works out for me?" And it begins again. *What we fear, we create.*

There's only one way to put a permanent stop to that cycle, and that's to declare a permanent moratorium on negative manifesting. No more. Period. To the extent that it's become a habit, make it just as much of a habit to immediately neutralize every moment of negative manifesting with an even more positive one until the positive ones become more of a habit and more powerful. Ask your family and friends to call you on it whenever they hear negative manifesting coming out of your mouth, and, by the way, do the same for them. My friends will back me up on this: I don't tolerate anyone in my presence being demeaning about themselves. And when I say I don't tolerate it, I mean I'll yell, "Stop that!" in the middle of their sentence if that's what it takes to get their attention. It's reciprocal too—my closest friends know to do exactly the same to me if they catch me slipping into old, destructive, negative manifesting habits.

What I've done now that I'm awake, and what I'm eager for you to do right along with me, is make the easy word transition from negative to positive manifesting and then keep reinforcing it in your mind until you accept it as the truth. Never forget, we *choose* the way we think and what we believe. We can only blame our childhoods and our parents for so long— after all, everything but murder has a statute of limitations, so we adults have to take responsibility for our own choices, celebrating the fact that they really are our choices now and, yes, we really are that powerful and that much in control over our own lives.

A few examples of that "easy word transition from negative to positive," just to get you started on a list of your own:

"I *will* be with a person who appreciates me, and nothing less."

"I *will* be with a person who treats me, and my emotions, with kindness, truth, and respect, and nothing less."

"I *will* be with a person who's supportive of my dreams, and nothing less."

"I *will* be with a person who's gentle with his words and actions, even if we're in an angry moment, and nothing less."

And, because there's no more essential relationship in our lives than the relationship we have with ourselves, let's add:

"I *will* find my own unique version of inner peace."

"I *will* find my own unique version of joy in my life."

"I *will* insist on a career that gives me satisfaction, stimulation, and a living that allows me to be proudly self-sufficient."

"I *will* strive every day to live my life in divine spiritual prosperity."

"I *will* live my life as an example of the very best of my beliefs."

Last but certainly not least, and you're hereby ordered to keep saying it until you really mean it:

"THERE IS NO ONE ELSE ON THIS EARTH I'D RATHER BE."

It really is that simple to turn negative manifesting into positive manifesting. But there's a Part 2 to the process of using this skill to change your life: *you have to do the work!* You can't just sit there manifesting all day without lifting a finger to make your dreams come true. Trust me, if I hadn't committed myself to countless singing lessons with the very best coach I could afford, and exhaustively prepared for the *Les Misérables* audition when it finally happened, I'd still be blathering away to that picture of Richard Jay-Alexander on my door, waiting for his imaginary phone call, long after his production of that beautiful show had come and gone from Broadway.

I know. It's hard to feel positive and motivated and hopeful when you're still reeling from the sting of a broken heart.

Here's the good news, though. Today's exercise can involve you enough both mentally and physically that you just might spend minutes at a time thinking more about yourself than about him. I want that for you! Why? Because he's not important anymore. *You* are. This is all about you, and, frankly, he's forfeited the honor of your company, your attention, and your celebration of your new, powerful, positively manifested life.

Today's Exercise

Back one more time to the picture of *Les Misérables* producer Richard Jay-Alexander on my door where I couldn't miss seeing it every day: I've expanded that literal example of positive manifesting into a collage board. It's not even close to an original idea, and if I could remember who first suggested it to me it would be my great pleasure to give them credit. For those of you who don't already know, all you need to invest in for a collage board is a bulletin board of whatever size you choose and plenty of pushpins or thumbtacks. Then, simply gather photographs, magazines, art supplies, anything and everything that inspires you, and start in. Your goal is nothing more and nothing less than a whole array of images that are reminders and manifestations of the very best of your dreams for the wonderful new life you're about to begin, happy, healthy, and heartbreaker-free.

For example, I made a mock cover for this book before I even had a literary agent, let alone a publisher, and put it on my collage board. I even added the words "Next Best Seller!" in one corner of the cover, partly because of course I'd love to be a best-selling author and partly because the more copies this book sells, the more heartbroken women are feeling a little more hopeful, a little more empowered, and a little less alone, I hope. Right next to the book cover is a picture of Oprah. I admit it, I talk to that picture every day, just like I talked to my picture of Richard Jay-Alexander, and tell it/her my intention that some-day I'll be sitting next to her on her legendary couch, probably crying like a baby in front of her bazillion viewers out of sheer gratitude that one of my longtime dreams is coming true. There are also pictures of my family all together and happy, a picture of my dream home, a mock script cover of a TV show I want to create, several photos of me at my most candid and genuinely joyful, and some of me at my most comfortable weight.

For the record, there's not a single shot of me and an ex-husband or ex-boyfriend. Not one of them are among my future dreams, and in each case if someone had told me I'd feel that way someday I would have laughed in their face. Which inspires me to add, as strongly as I can put it: pictures or any other representations of your heartbreaker are *strictly off limits!!! No exceptions, no excuses!!!* If it just so happens that your favorite joyful picture of yourself was taken when you were standing beside him, of course you can include that photo of yourself in your collage . . . after you get out the scissors and remove him from the shot. Whatever else you like is fair game

for your collage board, though, as long as it's a positive mani-
festation from your heart and, of equal importance, something
you're more than willing to work hard for. Have a good time,
be creative, be expansive, and keep adding to it, rearranging
it, playing with it—it is *yours*, after all, and I hope you'll also
take a moment every now and then to appreciate that yours
is as unique and singular as your dreams themselves. You are
that special, and don't you ever forget it.

If you're one of the many people to whom making a collage
board sounds too crafty for your taste, you can accomplish
the same thing with a list in your journal/diary/workbook. Instead of a collage board, call it a positive manifesting list. And
since a truly well-lived life is a perfect balance of the physical
and the spiritual, divide your list into two columns, one entitled Physical and one entitled Spiritual. For every physical
goal you write down—a new job, going back to school, appearing on *Oprah*, whatever—insist on writing a spiritual one
as well, like, "I will start each new day with a few moments of
gratitude," or, "Every day I will find an opportunity to extend
an act of kindness for no other reason than that it's right." As
with the collage board, let it be a work in progress, just as
you're a work in progress and so are we all.

Now, don't just sit there—go get started. And when you're finished, remember to put that *X* through Day 6 on your calendar.
I'm excited for you, my friend, and I'll meet you back here tomorrow. In the meantime, let me say it again—you're doing *great*!

DAY 7

Life 101

It is good to act as if. It is even better to grow
to the point where it is no longer an act.

—Charles Caleb Colton

I was between scenes on *One Life to Live* a couple of years ago when my friend Bob Bessoir, our brilliant lighting director, pulled me aside. He knew I'd just separated from my husband Michael and wanted to check on my pulse rate.

"How are you doing, Cat?" he asked.

"I'm doing great," I told him. "How are you?"

It was obvious from his reaction that he didn't believe me.

"It's amazing," I said, "but every morning the first thing I do when I wake up is tell myself, and *believe*, that life is great, and I'm great. And what do you know, my mind and soul seem to be buying it and following suit." Then I looked him squarely in the eyes and added, "In other words, fake it until you make it."

I'd heard that expression a million times, but I don't think

I really got it, really *knew* it, until that moment with Bob on the set.

Mind you, by that time I'd already been through a whole lot of tears, anger, and soul-searching. I'd spent countless hours trying to analyze what had gone wrong and how I'd arrived at this sad milestone in my life. In the years it took our marriage to crumble, I'd examined it under every microscope and magnifying glass I could get my hands on, and I finally understood my part in the demise of our fifteen years together as clearly as I understood his. I was honestly starting to feel gratitude for our ability to hang on to the deep friendship we'd built, and to believe that, with time, we could learn enough from the pain we'd caused each other to be better people for our newly defined relationship and for those unknown people we each might fall in love with someday.

There's no doubt about it, I wasn't exactly where I thought I'd be at that point in my life, but I was feeling occasional glimmers of being happy. I'd missed being happy. I'd missed who I am when I'm happy. I wanted and needed it to happen more often. So, unconsciously until that day on the set with Bob, I started faking it until I made it.

And the point is, it works.

Our minds really do follow directions quite beautifully.

Our minds can create either heaven on earth, or hell.

Our minds can make us braver, healthier, more adventurous, more capable, more fulfilled.

And our minds can convince us to live our lives scared to death.

When that starts to happen, just remember, there's nothing to be afraid of when it comes to affairs of the heart—as long as we apply all our attention, skills, and common sense when we do feel a few twinges of fear. Sometimes those feelings are nothing more than healthy warning signs to keep on moving without a single glance back. And sometimes they're stumbling blocks to our growth into vibrant, thriving, generous people who've learned to live with their eyes and hearts wide open.

If you talk to Char Margolis, or John Edward, or Sylvia Browne—and I have—they'll openly admit that they can't begin to predict what's going to happen in their personal lives. So if the most skilled psychics in the world aren't psychic about themselves, what on earth would make us think *we* are? Let's face it, we can't afford to indulge our whims and impulses and emotional irresponsibility anymore. We've done that, and look where it got us. We owe ourselves a commitment to learn everything we can about the signs and signals that tip us off to strong, positive, successful choices in our relationships and not settle for anything less, ever—not even for that minute or two when we're bored or lonely or feel like we want some attention or a distraction or someone new to get (momentarily) excited about.

I have a confession to make: I hated algebra when I was in school. I wasn't good at it, I didn't particularly aspire to be good at it, and, most of all, I couldn't imagine what the point was. And sure enough, do you know how many times I've had someone say at an audition, "You read those scenes beauti-

fully, Catherine, but can you tell us the square root of 722?"
Zero. Not once.

But do you know how many times I could have used some
courses in just plain Life 101 in my early years, and how many
disasters they could have saved me? I know, we have to live
life to really acquire useful knowledge about it, which is why
it's a fact that youth is wasted on the young. But wouldn't it be
wonderful if, in grades 1 to 12, kids were taught some of the
universal relationship laws and basic people-reading skills?
Wouldn't you have signed up for those in a heartbeat?

Here are just a few of the classes I'd have found so much
more useful than algebra under the general Life 101 category:

- Love 101
- You're Making Me Uncomfortable and Here's My
  Healthy Way of Handling It 101
- Laughter 101
- Joy 101
- Inner Peace 101
- Mind Your Own Business 101
- Knowing Who I Am 101
- There's No One Else on Earth I'd Rather Be 101

Can you imagine the length of the waiting lists for those
classes? Come to think of it, we don't have to imagine it. Dr.
Leo Buscaglia, best-selling author of several books on the
subject of love, actually taught a class at the University of
Southern California called Love 101. The USC administration

thought he was crazy when he pitched the idea. And he was—crazy like a fox. There was a waiting list a mile long to get into that class. Everyone was surprised except Dr. Leo Buscaglia.

He taught the principles of fearlessly loving yourself, and loving others more fully and fearlessly as a result. He taught how breaking down our own walls makes it possible to love ourselves unconditionally. He's my inspiration, and I'll always regret not doggedly pursuing a chance to meet him before he slipped out of his human suit into something more comfortable and divine.

Which is a perfect Life 101 lesson, by the way: don't get so busy or distracted that you inadvertently run out of time to pursue the dreams that matter.

I may not have satisfied my dream to meet Dr. Leo Buscaglia, but you're looking at a related dream, to continue his work in my own way. I don't have his body of experience to draw on. But I have mine, and it's my honor to share with you what I've discovered so far in this journey; I hope it speaks to you, and pray it helps you as it has helped me to find inner peace, and joy, no matter what's going on around you. As the saying goes, take what you need and leave the rest, and remember that not for one moment are you taking this trip alone.

Life 101 classes begin right here, wherever you're reading this, right now. No dress code, no grades, no pop quizzes, no time limit, no judgments, and *no algebra*. Just some earnest recommendations and exercises that I promise actually have a purpose, and, yes, you'll actually use them in real life. Here's a handful of the benefits of "graduating" from this course:

You get to be the boss of your own life.

You get to wake up every day knowing that you have the power to re-create your life into whatever you want it to be.

You get to make your dreams come true.

You get to feel peace and joy, because you *choose* to.

You get to throw out old beliefs that aren't serving you well and replace them with new ones that will inspire you to celebrate exactly who you are. Your new beliefs, especially about yourself, are going to be *yours*, and they're going to be nothing but positive, because they'll become your physical and emotional truth, I guarantee it.

Which leads me neatly to your Day 7 exercise, or, in this case, your Life 101 assignment:

You're going to wake up every morning starting tomorrow, acknowledge the grief you're temporarily (I promise) feeling just long enough to push through it, and then take your emotional temperature by asking and answering honestly, "What am I believing right now, and is it working for me or against me?"

Once you've devoted as many moments to that as you need, you're going to take the advice of the truly wonderful Joel Osteen in his book *Your Best Life Now*: you're going to say, out loud, with your voice and your heart:

Something really good is going to happen to me today.

That's it. Those two quick, easy assignments every single morning, the minute you wake up, until they become a habit. No more overthinking, no more underthinking. We're replacing those bad habits with these, to remind you of another essential lesson of Life 101:

Pure, healthy, simple thoughts fueled by powerful intentions are all you need to change your life.

You were born with a God-given right to joy. It's time to claim your birthright. One way or another you'll never forgive yourself if you settle for anything less.

Now, thank yourself for how splendidly you're doing.

See you tomorrow.

I'll be right here.

Today's Affirmation

I am healing, from the inside out, emerging a victor, in charge of my own life, my own happiness, and my own peace. The more sure I become of that, the more aware I am that love is available to me anytime I need it. Love multiplies itself the more it's given, even when I give it to myself. Others sense my love and are drawn to it like a light they want to be near, and I welcome those who will enhance my life and celebrate with me exactly who I am.

DAY 8

You're Making Me Uncomfortable

I am not afraid of storms, for I am learning how to sail my ship.

—Louisa May Alcott

Getting hurt is, to put it politely, the polar opposite of fun. Sometimes we inadvertently ask for it, by diving head-first into what by all appearances are shark-infested waters, thinking we'll either (a) simply love those sharks away or (b) convince ourselves that we can learn to love sharks.

Sometimes it's just the way things turn out.

No one makes it through life without getting hurt. The best we can do about that fact is to learn how, and if, we set ourselves up for it; to take an honest look at the ways in which we contributed to our own pain; make changes in ourselves (never forget—you'll never change anyone else, so let's all make a pact to give up that nonsense once and for all) that will help us choose more wisely in the future; and never forget to congratulate ourselves on how strong we are to have survived the hurt we've been through, and how much more strength we can gain from this current hurt.

After all, relationships are meant to *enhance* our lives. They're not meant to be nothing more than an endurance test. And when that's what they become, we have to acknowledge it and be smart enough to fearlessly do something about it. I'm not talking about those empty threats we've all been guilty of when we say, "If you don't stop (fill in unacceptable behavior that's hurting us), I'm leaving!" Six months later, when we're still there, and their behavior hasn't changed a bit, we might as well change the threat to, "If you don't stop (see above), I'm not going to do a thing about it!" I've said it before and I'll say it again, whether it's about us or about them: when there's any disparity between the words and the behavior, *believe the behavior.*

We've all been on both the giving and receiving ends of bad behavior. We're on a journey here toward our highest possible selves, and we learn the most from our missteps and our pain. So while you're not particularly feeling like celebrating at the moment, the good news is, you're a winner, in the midst of learning some very valuable lessons about yourself.

At some point or others in your life, I promise you've believed an untruth (or five, or ten, or a hundred) about yourself, projected onto you by someone else. It may have come from a partner, a colleague, a family member, or a friend. Where it comes from is beside the point. If you listened to it and took it in, it matters.

But once you've done a frank, thorough examination of

your own truth about yourself beyond all self-doubt, that truth that's ingrained in your soul, you'll recognize that others' opinions of you is only their perspective. That doesn't make it true. At best, it only makes it true for them, and based on what do they have more credibility about you than *you* do?

It's taken me more than fifty years to learn to listen to what I know about myself when it conflicts with what someone else is telling me what or who I *really* am, what and who I *really* should be, *really* should want, *really* should feel, and on and on and on. Unless it's positive and loving and supportive and a celebration of the person I've worked very hard to become, it's finally starting to sound to me like nothing more than a lot of projecting and blathering.

In other words, I finally got tired of trying to be comfortable with being uncomfortable. And I want you to get tired of it too, and trade it for the mind-set of a winner. A champion.

Winners surround themselves with winners, and they can't be bothered with those who wish anything less than the best. Winners find, and become, teammates everywhere they go so that there's no manipulative negativity to slog through just to get through a day, no other agenda than the best they can be. If some part of you is wondering if it really makes that much of a difference, ask yourself if you've ever heard an Olympic gold medalist or an Academy Award winner stand at the microphone and say, "I'd like to thank my significant other for reminding me every day what an insensitive, stupid, inept, disappointing, neglectful bitch I am." Winners know they can't emotionally afford that nonsense. And neither can we.

It's safe to say that most of us have tried to slog our way through relationships with perpetual victims, aka blamers, in our lives. They are the people who believe in their heart of hearts that everyone's out to get them, nothing ever goes right, they can't get the breaks they so richly deserve, no one truly understands them, and everything that's wrong in their lives is someone else's fault (including yours). Yawn.

Mind you, at the beginning of the relationship they very probably offered lovely "responsibility" speeches and sincere-sounding apologies for arguments and bad behavior. Otherwise, why would we have fallen for them? But ônce deeper commitments are made, here come the controlling insults and undermining swipes at our self-confidence, because (a) God forbid we should have enough pride and integrity to walk away with an appropriate, "Get lost!" and (b) how else can they shift the blame for their unhappiness onto us, where they'll convince us it belongs if we let them?

The one and only thing the blamer is consistently accurate about is that, indeed, nothing ever really does go right for them. Why? All together now: *because that's what they believe, and they'll trample on anyone who stands in the way of making it true!*

Let's face it, we've occasionally slipped into the role of blamer or victim ourselves from time to time.

We've accepted utterly unacceptable behavior.

We've compromised our priorities to put a stop to someone else's complaints about us.

We've twisted ourselves into pretzels trying to make sense

out of someone else's nonsense, order out of someone else's chaos, romance out of someone else's melodrama, and peace out of someone else's battle mentality.

Ultimately, we've tried, in desperate futility, to be comfortable with our own uncomfortability. (I know. The proper word is "discomfort." But it doesn't seem to have quite the same impact.) We've suppressed, or even scolded ourselves for, our uncomfortability to the point where we've suffered the physical and emotional consequences of tolerating the intolerable: headaches, backaches, stomachaches, extreme weight gain or loss, perpetual anger, confusion, sadness, depression . . . the list goes on and on. And for what? So that tomorrow we can put up with it all over again rather than make someone unhappy who seems to have their heart set on it anyway? Please.

Here's just a small sampling of comments a blamer is likely to resort to in an effort to "keep us in our place":

"You're so self-centered!"
"Stop being so sensitive, I was just kidding!"
"You never listen!"
"You just don't care!"
"I want to get to the bottom of what's wrong with you!"
"I swear you're schizophrenic!"
"I just want to know where my girlfriend went, because you're certainly not her!"
"You're not the same person I fell in love with!"

Don't you just love a sweet-talker?

But those are perfect opportunities to pause—and I do mean *pause*, for as long as we want and need—and take a good look at that truth we talked about, that we know with absolute certainty about ourselves, and see if it matches their truth about us.

Am I self-centered?

Am I hypersensitive?

Do I listen?

Etc.

If their "truth" about us truly doesn't match our own, when we know we've just heard an untruth about ourselves, remember: if we know ourselves and our truths well enough and deeply enough, there's no reason to defend ourselves in the face of overt or covert untruths. There's no argument to be had. There's nothing worth responding to, beyond a simple, "That's not true, but I'm sorry you feel that way."

Of course, the human knee-jerk reaction is to leap immediately into reactor mode, with some variation of, "No, I'm not!"—virtually guaranteed to inspire a few pitiful junior-high-level rounds of "Are too!" "Am not!" that aren't worth the oxygen it takes to say them. The alternative is a version of, "Why do you think that about me?" The downside of that, obviously, is that it invites an answer to something that has no basis in fact to begin with, not to mention the fact that it engages you in a conversation that implies you think they may have some basis for the insult or accusation—*which you know in your soul they don't, if you'll just pause and evaluate your own truth instead of reacting!*

Remember, reacting means being controlled by someone else's emotions while losing control of our own. It's a surefire way to get lured into a debate that's already designed to put us on the defensive, when we're hardly at our best, brightest, and most articulate. And it's a setup to be involved in another person's game you never asked to play in the first place, where the deck is stacked against you in such a way that you can't possibly win.

I've learned, the hard way, that the game can only go on if I let it, and I'm done playing games I can't win. Again, simply say (don't ask), "That's not true, but I'm sorry you feel that way." Or tell them to take a time-out and you'll get back to them. Let's face it, if adults are going to behave like children, a time-out is in perfectly reasonable order. Then, while they stand there sputtering, or storming around the room making victim noises, or throwing themselves into a chair in sheer exasperation at how impossible and unreasonable you are (because you're not playing the way you're supposed to), collect yourself and your thoughts and luxuriate in the knowledge that you haven't bought into an untruth about yourself, you haven't reduced yourself to behavior you find unattractive if not ridiculous, and you haven't invested several precious minutes/hours/months/years of your life trying to figure out a rational response to irrational, accusatory blather. Or, as a friend of mine calls it, "barking."

What you *have* done is the essence of this chapter: you've refused to be comfortable anymore with uncomfortability. Respect it to the extent that you pay attention to it and take action on it, but not for one more minute will you tolerate getting comfortable with it.

Some of you have already figured all this out, and believe me, the rest of us salute you. For those who haven't, your exercise is the same thing you apply to every other new skill: practice, practice, practice.

You don't need to wait for your next relationship to come along (and it will, if you want it to, in case you're still wondering). You can try this new skill with people you're in contact with every day, and slowly but surely make great strides in the way you relate to the world around you, and to yourself.

All you have to do is *really listen* to what people say to you. When it's something about yourself that you know to be untrue, *don't react immediately*. Take a deep breath, get calm, gather your power, and control and respond with the two un-provocative choices we've talked about: "That's not true, but I'm sorry you feel that way," or a simple, "I'll have to get back to you on that." You'll love the calm, you'll love the clarity, you'll love the time and frustration it saves, and, even if it's only subconsciously, you'll love learning to refuse to accept even the slightest wounds at a time when you're working so hard on healing.

For the record, not for a moment am I suggesting that you track down your heartbreaker, who very probably dished out his share of uncomfortability while you were together, and flex the muscles of this new response/skill you're working on. That's over with. He's yesterday's news. You're moving on, moving forward, with new self-knowledge, new skills, and a deep new appreciation of who you are that cannot and will not be compromised. After all, love is not a license for someone to be unkind, to manipulate and control by battering away at you with untruths and erode your self-esteem.

Love enhances.

Love celebrates and cherishes who you are.

Anything less is unacceptable.

Now, open your journal/diary/workbook to the first blank page and write down, as many times as it takes to make them yours, your two new mantras in the face of attempted insults:

That's not true, but I'm sorry you feel that way.
I'll have to get back to you on that.

Then simply promise yourself that whichever of those you use from now on will be the official end to a conversation that by definition has already outlived its usefulness anyway.

And a quick but meaningful P.S.—

Pay close attention to how the next "he" (and everyone else close to you as well) behaves in society in general. If he talks down to waitresses, clerks, or valets; if no restaurant table is ever good enough; if he speaks ill of his mother or his friends behind their backs; if he puts down women or any other generalized cultural group, even if he's "just joking" (yeah, right) . . .

Recognize that twinge of uncomfortability you're feeling, and respect it for the warning sign it's giving you that this is how he treats people and if you stick around, sooner or later that's exactly the treatment you have to look forward to.

Then, just one more mantra to write down and memorize for future reference: ***No, thank you, and bye-bye.***

Today's Affirmation

I have the courage to look inside my soul and learn everything that's true about myself. From this moment on I will stay calm amidst the nonsense of others so that I can think clearly and never again let anyone else determine my opinion of myself. I create the life I dream of by fearlessly standing up for who I am and who I continue to become, in the name of inner peace.

DAY 9

Shattering Illusions

Who looks outside, dreams. Who looks inside, awakens.

—Carl Jung

Illusions can be the prettiest little distractions, can't they? Unfortunately, they can also be among the most relationship-confusing, fear-inducing, self-defeating mental exercises we put ourselves through in our day-to-day lives. Just think how liberating it would be to learn to tell illusion from reality and shatter every one of those illusions we've created that aren't serving us well.

One of the areas of illusion you're probably struggling with right now has everything to do with your heartbreaker—what a great guy he was, how incomplete your life will be without him, how much fun he was, how beautifully he treated you, how generous he was, how interested he was in the things that matter to you, how supportive he was of your priorities, what a great listener he was . . . Believe me, I know. Our dreamy, romanticized memories about our heartbreakers can go on and on for pages, and what's hilarious is, if we're brutally honest with ourselves, we know perfectly well that most of those memories are nothing *but* illusions. Which means we haven't even let our hearts be broken by the real thing, we've let them be broken by figments of our imagination. And very often, I swear, it's not him we're having so much trouble letting go of, it's our *illusions* of him. I'm not sure if we cling so fiercely to the illusions of him because it's the only way we can justify what we put ourselves through to make him happy, or if it's because we're confusing our illusions with all that potential we saw in him that we just knew we could inspire him to achieve. Either way, if we can shatter those illusions and see through the shards to who he really was and how he really treated us, let's say, 98.5 percent of the time, there's a very good chance that we'll find it so much easier to move on. And what do you know, we might even be better off without him! Even if you don't find that to be completely true yet, the good news is that while you can't control him (or anyone else) for a single second, you can control your ability to develop the skill of shattering illusions to make way for reality.

And then there's the illusion that has become a bad habit for most of us at one time or another: the illusion of fear. It's true, fear is the foundation upon which many of our illusions are built, a collage of imagery that usually combines a few fragments of what we know with a whole lot of things we make up to fill in the blanks. Fear of living, fear of dying, fear of success, fear of failure, fear of falling in love, fear of being alone, fear of rejection, fear of commitment because our past has made it so hard to trust ourselves in the future—not one of those fears is even possible without our imaginations creating the vast majority of the details. The question is, since we're imagining so much of the eventuality we're afraid of, why not simply make it a habit to imagine a positive outcome instead and save ourselves a lot of anticipatory anxiety?

Obviously, a little fear is valuable, when it's genuine instinct, warning us of potential danger. But in general, fear is the opposite of faith, and it perpetuates the illusion that we're never quite safe, never quite capable, never quite enough, never quite just fine, thank you. And what a terrible disservice to do to ourselves, and to reinforce day after day, as our fears feed on themselves and our illusions take control of us rather than the other way around.

Remember, the word "fear" is an acronym for False Evidence Appearing Real—a perfect definition of illusion when you think about it.

Here are some "statements of fact" (read, illusions) I frequently hear from single girlfriends on the subject of meeting someone new:

"All the good ones are taken."
"I'm awkward with people I don't know."
"I'm a magnet for every lunatic in the room."
"You can't trust anyone these days."

Now, you'll never hear me advocate throwing caution and common sense to the wind when it comes to relationships, but there's a difference between caution and negative, fear-based illusions, and every one of those examples crosses that line. They limit our lives rather than enhance them. They encourage emotional paralysis rather than growth. They make assumptions based on self-manufactured illusions about ourselves, our past, and a whole world full of people we've never even met. And they project a lot of our "issues" (I try to avoid that overused word as much as possible, but when it fits, it fits) onto perfect strangers who've done nothing to deserve them (yet).

But probably the biggest reason I want to talk about the danger of illusions is that at this painful time in your life, when your heart has been broken, you're probably falling into a trap I'm all too familiar with: bombarding yourself with illusions that are guaranteed to make you feel even worse, and guaranteed to be nothing more than your overactive, wounded imagination. See if any of these sound familiar:

"I guess I wasn't (smart, successful, sexy, pretty, exciting) enough for him."

"If I'd tried harder, he wouldn't have broken up with me."

"I loved him as best I could and he still didn't want me."

"If he'd just tell me what I did wrong, I know I could make it up to him."

"I must not be worth loving."

"I'll never love anyone as much as I loved him."

Now, how do I know those are all illusions? Because I've told myself every one of those things in some form or other during the grief of a breakup. I believed them to be the absolute truth, and all the proof I thought I needed was that he didn't want me anymore. It was only after time had passed and I'd done some healing and had more perspective that I woke up and realized that if someone's not bright enough to appreciate who I am and what I have to offer, it really doesn't matter whether or not he wants me—*I don't want him!* And exclusively blaming myself for the downfall of a two-person relationship? How could that be anything but an illusion?

One of my favorite illustrations of how mistaken illusions can be when we'd be willing to bet we're right is the story of the four blindfolded men meeting an elephant for the first time and being asked to describe it. The man who reached up and felt the tail announced, "An elephant is like a rope." The man who felt the leg argued, "Are you crazy? An elephant is like a tree stump." The man whose hands were wrapped around the trunk said, "You're both delusional. An elephant is like a hose." And the man who was feeling the massive side replied, "I don't know what any of you are talking about. An elephant is obviously like a huge leathery wall."

All of them right, all of them wrong. And obviously the only way they were finally able to accurately describe an elephant—to shatter their individual illusions about what an elephant looks like—was to take off their blindfolds and step back for an objective look at the whole thing.

Trust me, I'm still just as capable as ever of being blindfolded, whether it's about relationships or work or family or just plain old life. The difference is that over the years I've learned to catch myself at indulging in illusions and snap myself out of it with a single-word command:

"Identify!"

That's my cue to take off the blindfold, stop telling myself that an elephant is like a rope or a tree stump, and step back for some good old objectivity and perspective.

Which leads me neatly to . . .

Today's Exercise

At the very moment you find yourself feeling anxious, or afraid, or angry, or sad, or inadequate, or not worth loving, I want you to say, out loud, the word, "Identify!"

I don't care if it makes you feel silly or crazy. Just do it.

It's your reminder that you've put that blindfold on again, and you're not looking at the whole elephant. You're getting lost in illusions and losing perspective. It's your reminder that the big picture is very different, and undoubtedly much more accurate, than the isolated image you've focused on.

"Identify!" is your reminder to stand back, become an objective observer of what's going on in your mind, what happened in that exact moment when the anxiety or sadness or fear or feeling of inadequacy crashed into you.

With your blindfold off, figure out what triggered that moment—and when you make it an issue, you'll be amazed at how quickly you were able to identify the trigger. Write it down, immediately or as soon as you can get to your journal/ diary/workbook. If nothing else, using "Identify!" as a cue to focus on what triggered your feeling badly is a brilliant way to cut through that swirling, chaotic think-mess in your head, simplify your thoughts, and smile at how quickly you're learning never to fall into that useless, destructive illusion trap again.

Today's Affirmation

I am ready to shatter my illusions. If my mind starts creating illusions that make me feel like anything less than the kind, loving, beautiful, capable, generous soul I know I am I'll stop myself, connect to my inner peace, say "Identify!" and watch those illusions vanish into thin air where they belong.

DAY 10

Whose Reality Is It Anyway?

When things go wrong, don't go with them.

—Anonymous

At some time or other, nearly all of us fall into the trap of being codependent.

I'm a recovering codependent myself.

I know what it's like to take on someone else's feelings as my own. To actually believe it's my job to solve their issues, to fix things for them, to make their business mine, to spend the majority of my time in their head rather than mine. I'm painfully familiar with the mistaken belief that part of loving someone is making their life my number one priority and wearing myself out trying to choreograph, orchestrate, and facilitate it for them—both of us throwing all our effort into making him happy. I have vast expertise in being so busy trying to convince him to want me that I forget to pay attention to whether or not I want him.

I called myself "generous" for it. "Caring." "Thoughtful." "Cooperative." "Sensitive." My particular favorite, "empathetic."

Nope. Sorry. Just codependent.

I said to my therapist once while recovering from an especially rough heartbreak in which I'd lost myself as usual for the sake of devoting myself to him, "I guess I thought if I treated him beautifully one hundred percent of the time no matter how he treated me, there would turn out to be some sort of payoff for that."

To which he replied, "You think they should hand out medals for masochism?"

It made me smile. I answered, "No, I certainly don't." I meant it, and I thank him for that rhetorical question, that kick in the butt, to this very day, as I continue to work on breaking the codependency habit. I'm tired of it. I'm tired of making myself crazy from it. I'm tired of "making up the difference" in my own imagination for men who really weren't even right for me in the first place if I took a good, objective look. But what card-carrying codependent wants to take a good, objective look at the men we're with, when we're so busy absorbing ourselves in them and calling it a life?

If any of this sounds even slightly familiar to you, please, come right on in, kick off your shoes, curl up by the fire, and make yourself comfortable. You're in good, loving, understanding company—company that's not here to wallow in this behavior and make excuses for it, but to walk our way out of it together with our heads held high, because there's a lot to be proud of in refusing to accept the unacceptable, even in ourselves.

It's taken me three very significant relationships to get this tired of it. And all three of them started pretty much the same way, which you'd think might have helped me recognize familiar territory a little sooner. But no. I couldn't know what I didn't know, and we all learn our own lessons in our own time, at our own pace.

(I'm suddenly reminded of that great definition of insanity: repeating the same behavior over and over again and expecting a different outcome.)

We'll fast-forward through the oh-so-adorable meeting/first date/attraction/giddy/no-basis-in-reality-while-pretending-we-know-exactly-what-we're-doing process and cut straight to a few weeks or months down the line.

I would sit and listen to him talk about his problems and frustrations, usually involving a "lack" of some kind in their situation. My knee-jerk reaction: to take on their anxiety as if it were my own, with the accompanying urgent feeling that I had to *do* something about it. Inevitably, of course, my own needs and responsibilities and other important relationships in my life would be neglected in the process. In fact, my ability to even concentrate on anything but him, what he needed, and how I could satisfy it would become virtually nonexistent.

Also, inevitably, I'd start to resent it, him, and myself. But I could push those thoughts of resentment aside so quickly it was as if they never existed. After all, I was trying to build a life with this man. A *future*. Sacrifice and compromise are essential parts of building a relationship, right? (What's that? Only one of us was doing all the sacrificing and compromising? Sorry, I can't be bothered to discuss that right now, I'm in love.)

In rare moments of clarity and self-worth I'd take a step or two toward my own priorities. But a simple comment from him like, "You just don't care," or the slightly more hostage-holding, "If you really cared about me, you'd (fill in completely self-serving comment)," and I'd be off to the races again, throwing my own business into the back of the closet again and leaping headfirst back into his again.

It made me feel perpetually exhausted, physically and emotionally, and perpetually anxious as well, since no matter what I was doing, if it wasn't directly concerned with him somehow, I felt as if I was being selfish. And I couldn't really place the blame on him. I habitually did it to myself. I habitually made the choice to step yet again into my Super Girlfriend costume, with tights and cape, legs spread apart and hands on hips: "Here I come to save the daaaaaaaaay!"

(Always recognize it as a dim light of hope, by the way, when you just can't manage to shift the responsibility for your ridiculous behavior to anyone but yourself. Thank you again, Dr. Phil. *You can't change what you don't acknowledge.*)

Another great talent of the true codependent is the ability to ignore red flags, and I was especially adept at that with one of these men in particular. One of the first things I thought attracted me to him was what I euphemistically called his "adorable childlike qualities." Translation, I discovered: he was just plain childish. He had other perfectly nice qualities, though, so surely I could overlook childishness, couldn't I? Like how he was only happy when he had me all to himself? Or how he would pout and whine when we weren't doing what he wanted to do? (Mind you, I wouldn't tolerate that nonsense for five minutes in an actual child, but I was making excuses for it in a grown man!)

He started pretty early in the relationship putting words in my mouth, quoting things I knew for certain I never said but swearing I had.

In the meantime, inappropriate and sometimes even cruel things would pop out of his mouth (I almost said "when he felt insecure," but that would be a codependent, excusing-it thing to say, wouldn't it?), which he always immediately followed with, "I can't believe I said that," as if that made anything and everything he said acceptable.

He had very few friends. Never a good sign.

He was unhappy with where he was in his career. And in case I forgot for a minute or two that that was the case, he was right there with constant, endless monologues about it. Listening never seemed like enough. I invariably felt as if I had to do something. Right away. Surely I knew someone who could help, or knew someone who knew someone, or, or, or . . . (By the way, I don't remember that I'd ever been happier with where I was in *my* career, but that subject and any celebration of it were off-limits. How dare I make an issue of things going well for me until/unless they were going as well or better for him, right?)

He had a rough childhood. Codependent heaven. I had a rough childhood too. (Of course, I let the statute of limitations run out on mine years ago and refuse to let myself wallow in it, so the obvious question could be asked: why was I helping him wallow in his and trying impossibly to make up the difference? I hadn't arrived at the obvious answer yet, that it wasn't my job, and that if I could grow into a kind, responsible, hardworking, generous adult, he sure as hell had that choice too.)

He continually lectured me on what would make things "better for us," continually raising the bar, and predictably it was always some change or effort I needed to make. (Cue Super Girlfriend costume.) I couldn't imagine that someone who claimed to love me would expect something more of me than was fair and reasonable, so (huff, huff, puff, puff) I would meet that bar every time . . . only to discover that, no, that hadn't made it better for us after all, because now there was a *new* issue. I was in a constant lose-lose; damned if I did, damned if I didn't; "you're such a disappointment" situation. But does codependent Super Girlfriend draw boundaries and ever say anything but yes? I don't think so.

Needless to say, running his race, wrestling with his problems, absorbing his feelings and struggles, trying to mitigate his frustrations, feeling virtually blackmailed into praising anything and everything he did because the pouting when I didn't wasn't worth it, always trying but never hard enough according to my nonstop reviews, invariably cooperating when it came to what we were going to do and the lack of friends we were going to do it with inevitably stressed me out, wore me down, made me angry and resentful behind a smile of horribly strained patience, and, ultimately, literally made me sick. I developed massive headaches. I gained weight. I was eating in a way I hated and doing things I had no interest in doing. In other words, just as I'd given up the idea of drawing boundaries with him, I abandoned boundaries for myself as well, and that's a sure path to absolutely nowhere.

If you're wondering where my friends were during all this, they were nearby, available and loving me; it's just that I didn't want to discuss any of this with them because I didn't want them not to like my boyfriend. After all, I just *knew* he would come to his senses any minute now and stop acting out. After all, I'd been such an inspiration, such a loving and devoted partner, so unflinchingly and adoringly *helpful.* Oh, brother . . .

Finally, like an unopened soda bottle that's been violently shaken, my unexpressed emotions blew, and blew big. He didn't know what hit him. He hadn't been called on a single thing since the moment I met him because I didn't want to hurt his feelings. Never mind that mine were being hurt constantly. I had cast myself in the perfect codependent martyr role . . . and sacrificed myself in the process. Which I would never forgive myself for if I hadn't made a promise to myself to never, ever let it happen again.

No, the end of this story isn't that he saw the error of his ways, apologized, made a complete 180-degree turnaround, and we're still together to this very day. I frankly don't even think that would qualify as a happy ending, because looking back, I don't even think we were ever going to be each other's dream come true. The end of this story is that I let the relationship go, and I did it fair and clean and healthy, wishing him all the best . . . somewhere else, with someone else. I hurt his feelings, but here's the headline—not a *fraction* as much as I'd have hurt him if I'd kept on tolerating and keeping my mouth shut and being, let's face it, about as dishonest as it gets in an affair of the heart, where dishonesty is fatal.

So, now that we've sworn off dishonesty, here's just some of the truth I came away with, from that relationship and a couple of others that were all too similar:

If we don't refuse to ignore and make excuses for our codependency, we'll keep acting it out again and again and again, sometimes for no other reason than the saddest one of all: it feels familiar.

I was not the victim of that relationship. I chose it, sleepwalking every step of the way, and never doubt that we really are the sum total of our own choices. He didn't make me sacrifice myself. I did that all by myself, by never drawing a single boundary, by saying things were okay with me when they weren't at all, by using him instead of myself as the yardstick by which I was measuring my own growth. He wasn't trying to drive me crazy, he just *was*. He wasn't trying to hurt me, he just *was*. And you know what? He gets to be himself, whoever he is. And I get to choose whether who he is complements my life or contaminates it. The latter happened to be the case, but I had no business taking so long to say no, thanks and good-bye.

"Putting up a front," as I did for the friends and family who truly love me and have my best interests at heart, was just another way of sacrificing myself for him. When I finally started opening up to them again, they had such valuable perspective, context, and just plain support to offer. Don't work without a net for one more minute.

The most loving thing we can do for ourselves and for those we love is to keep our hearts open to them without exchanging our hearts for theirs. Let their feelings and their challenges be theirs, just as you insist that your feelings and your challenges be yours. Mind your business, and pay attention to how—and if—they mind theirs. Crisis doesn't build character, the saying goes, it reveals it. When what gets revealed is weakness, laziness, and chronic whining while running in place, don't play the codependent trick on yourself that you'll simply do it for them. That's not how you inspire strength; it's how you cripple a soul.

Last but certainly not least: in any relationship, no one else's feelings are ever more important than yours. One more time: *no one else's feelings are ever more important than yours.*

Take it from a reformed codependent. If I can make it out of that trap, you can too, and I promise, it's wonderful out here!

Instead of an exercise, today you're going to do . . .

Heartwork

I shared a relationship story with you in this chapter. Now I want you to share one with yourself. Get out your journal and write down, as I did, the truth about him and about you in the relationship that's left you feeling heartbroken. When you get into those details that make you sad, resentful, angry, and unhealthy, go right ahead and feel every one of those things. Then remind yourself that you chose all of it, and you did it so you could learn and grow and keep a promise to yourself that you'll never, ever sacrifice yourself like that again.

Now, let it all go with a long, joyful breath and step into a whole new level of gratitude.

Let the drama go, give yourself a hug from me, and say thank you.

DAY 11

What's the Prize?

Trust your hopes, not your fears.

—David Mahoney

A few years ago I ran into a colleague I hadn't seen since her network job took her to another state the year before. She's a lovely, successful woman with a wonderful sense of humor, and I always appreciated how happy she seemed to be in a business full of whiners. She'd confided in me more than once that, grateful as she was for how well her life was going in general, her greatest wish was to meet someone, fall in love, and marry her own version of Prince Charming. I didn't doubt for a moment that it would happen for her: she had so much to offer the right man, or, as I often put it, so much to bring to the barbecue.

So I wasn't one bit surprised when, within a year of starting her new life in a new city, she met the man of her dreams. Or so she thought . . .

She loved him, and after two years in a committed relationship, she felt that things between them were just fine. Unfortunately, "just fine" wasn't her lifelong dream, any more than it should be yours or mine. She wanted to marry him and make a home and a life with him. He, on the other hand, seemed to be dragging his feet and never implied that marrying her was anywhere to be found on his must-do list.

Finally, believing that knowing is always better than not knowing, and tired of overanalyzing every word that came out of his mouth about their relationship, she decided it was time for them to have That Talk. She lit candles, ordered in his favorite food (cooking was not among her talents, and she had the decency to admit it), slipped into some filmy Victoria's Secret number, and addressed the subject as she poured him a beveled crystal glass of hilariously expensive merlot. (Come on, I've done my version of exactly the same thing and so have you.) She clearly spelled out how much she loved him, how happy she'd been in their two years together, and how she needed to know if her hope that their relationship was leading toward marriage was his hope as well.

His response was an only slightly more eloquent version of no. He wasn't being cruel, just as honest and straightforward as she deserved. Marriage had never been a priority of his, with her or with anyone else. He wasn't ready for such a serious commitment, and he couldn't promise her that he ever would be.

She was devastated, angry, and confused. She'd loved him as best she could, given him her all, been more devoted and attentive to him than to anyone else in her life. According to her emotional logic, that was supposed to lead to a wedding sooner or later, not just flat-line into the limbo of a lifelong boyfriend. And she certainly wasn't about to apologize for a perfectly reasonable dream. So she gave him an ultimatum: if he wasn't willing to commit to marrying her sometime in the foreseeable future, she would have to end their relationship and move on.

He wasn't. She moved on, heartbroken.

It was a month or so later that I ran into her. She put on her best smile, but it was obvious she'd somehow lost her spark since I'd last seen her, as if her pilot light had burned out.

I hugged her and cheerfully asked, "How are you?" as if I hadn't already guessed.

"Terrible," she answered. "My life is garbage." (She used a different word.)

We were at a huge, noisy network party, surrounded by hundreds of colleagues in cocktail wear. I took her hand and led her to the relative privacy of a stairwell, where she told me the story of ending her relationship with Mr. Right.

When she finished, I'm sure I threw her a little, and probably sounded insensitive, as I spontaneously hugged her again and said, "Good for you!"

She couldn't imagine what she'd done to inspire praise. "Good for me? For what?" she asked.

"For knowing what you want and refusing to settle for anything less. For not telling yourself that lie that if you stuck around long enough you could change his mind. For freeing yourself up to fall in love with someone who wants the same thing you do out of a relationship."

She wasn't convinced, but she wasn't telling me to shut up, either, which I invariably take as a cue that whoever I'm talking to is open to hearing the rest of what I have to say. "Great," she said, fighting back tears. "I did the right thing. So why does the right thing have to hurt so much?"

I'd learned the answer to that one the hard way, many times. "Because you're grieving the loss of a relationship you completely invested in and a man you were hoping to spend the rest of your life with. And that grief is excruciating. But I promise, the day will come when you realize that losing a man who doesn't want to make a commitment to you is no loss at all. In the meantime, be proud of yourself for not compromising your dreams."

She didn't say anything, but I saw a faint smile and a brief flicker of light in her eyes, and this time she initiated the hug. As I held on to her and hoped she was drawing some strength from my sincere belief in her, I couldn't resist adding, "And by the way, don't ever let me hear you say again that your life is garbage. Saying it is reinforcing it, and reinforcing it leads to creating it. Your life is as precious and beautiful as you're willing to make it."

We made our way back to the party, and just before we were swallowed up into the sea of air kisses and network politics I asked her to please keep in touch and, if she wanted, let me "heartbreak-cure" her. She enthusiastically agreed, then disappeared into the crowd.

Another two years passed without my hearing a peep out of her. I never push, ever, so I let it go at that and hoped her silence meant that she hadn't needed heartbreak-busting after all, because she was happy, healthy, and thriving in her decision to move on from the man who didn't care to commit.

And then, along came another network party, where I ran into one of our mutual colleagues. I asked about her. Ready? She'd gone back to him. They still weren't married or even talking about it. And here's a surprise: she wasn't very happy.

I wasn't shocked. I wasn't throwing stones either. I've settled for less than my dreams in the name of love too, and discovered that it's one sure way to destroy the joy in your life, not to mention wasting valuable space in your heart that could be so much better filled by someone whose dreams are compatible with yours.

And you and I both know what she would say if I called and asked her why she went back to a man who'd already made it crystal clear that he wouldn't be making one of her most treasured dreams come true. All together now: "Because I love him!" I swear, we have got to stop using that lame excuse to explain away our bad choices. It's become sort of a catchall euphemism for "If I blame it on love, then I don't have to take responsibility for it," and in the end that's not only untrue, it's potentially disastrous. We all need to remember that "because I love him" is often the cliché behind everything from tolerating abuse to endangering children around Mommy's new ex-con boyfriend, and it's no more legitimate as an excuse for staying with someone who's already stated very clearly, in some form or other, "I am *not* the answer to your prayers."

I don't know how much more clearly the man in my friend's

situation could have put it than, "I don't want to make a commitment and I'm not sure I ever will." In fact, when you think about it, he was a lot more honest than she was—and again, I'm not throwing stones. I've been her, in this same situation. What he said, with crystal clarity was, "No marriage potential here, but thank you for playing our game." What she said was, "If you won't promise to marry me someday, I'm leaving," after which, following a brief hiatus, she went back. And what compromises our credibility and dignity faster than an ultimatum we don't stick to?

So as you prepare to march proud and healthy back into the world of relationships, memorize and repeat two or three hundred times a day the following bit of wisdom:

Say what you mean and mean what you say, and assume unless there's evidence to the contrary that he's doing the same.

As for that pesky "evidence to the contrary," it's much simpler than we often make it. It boils down to nothing more than this: when his words don't match his actions, believe the actions, every time. Anyone can pretty much say anything to anyone, but with no behavior to back up what's said, the words themselves are meaningless. On the other hand, when the words and actions match perfectly—as in, "I have no intention of marrying you now or ever, and if marriage is important to you we shouldn't be together," followed by his making a break for the nearest exit—take them to heart as the truth and act accordingly.

Sadly, you and I both know, probably because we've been there, what it's costing my friend to maintain the relationship she went back to and why she's not happy. She's either hard at work convincing herself that her lifelong dream of being married someday isn't that important or is more than she deserves, or she's hard at work trying to "fix" him and inspire him to want to marry her after all. Whichever of those she's chosen, she's letting her self-esteem slip further and further into obscurity with every passing day. I'm not sure which is more destructive: "My dreams don't matter," or "Every day I don't manage to change his mind is another day in which I've failed." Isn't that sad, and just a terrible way to live?

Promise yourself that from now on, you're going to keep your eye on the prize and nothing less. The prize is *not* someone whose primary life goals are in direct conflict with yours. The prize is *not* someone with whom your self-esteem is compromised, either deliberately or because you set yourself up for it. The prize is *not* someone you believe you might be happy with someday, after you've "fixed" him. The prize is *not* someone you go back to under the theory that "someone is better than no one." (A theory that happens to be completely untrue, by the way.)

The prize has life goals that are compatible with yours. The prize wants to participate in making your dreams a reality, rather than making you feel inappropriate for having them. The prize celebrates who you are so that your self-esteem can thrive and soar, and he inspires you to be even better than you already are. The prize says what he means and means what he says. The prize is more healthy than painful in your life. The prize enhances your life, rather than simply complicating it. And the prize is most definitely worth making room for and waiting for, while refusing to settle for anything less.

Today's Exercise

Today's assignment is about making room for the prize. No, he's not your heartbreaker, for all the reasons we've discussed and plenty more you're well aware of if you'll be brutally honest with yourself. The prize is up ahead, not back there, but he can't come into your life if there's no space available because you haven't cleared it for him yet.

I happen to love what I think of as the cup metaphor, which illustrates the point clearly, simply, and perfectly. Don't just picture this. Do it. It will have more impact that way, and I want you to get the most benefit out of every day we're spending together.

First, get a cup—a teacup, a measuring cup, any cup that's handy.

Fill that cup to the brim with water and place it on a nice clean counter.

Now, pour more water into it.

I know. It can't be done, because the cup is already too full to allow any new water to replace the old.

In fact, all you accomplished was causing the cup to overflow and making a mess on your nice clean counter.

That full cup, of course, is you, until you release yourself from the bondage of sadness and anger left over from trying to build a relationship with someone who, by definition, wasn't the prize you deserve. Remember, the universe can't bring you your heart's desire until you make room for it. My friend obviously didn't empty her cup during her time away from the man who didn't commit. You and I know he's not her prize. He may be someone else's prize, but he's certainly not hers. And let's face it, no matter how hard she might be trying, she's not his prize either, or he never would have let her go in the first place.

So every time you think you're missing your heartbreaker and wish you were together again, head straight back to that cup and repeat today's exercise. Then ask yourself if your dreams, and the prize who sincerely wants to be part of them, don't deserve a lot better than being nothing but a mess on your counter.

Of course they do!

Today's Affirmation

Today I will empty my cup. I am doing this to make room for what I truly want and truly need in my life. I am enough just as I am, and I don't need to compromise or apologize to be worthy of someone's love. I trust in the universe that if I desire a lover in my life, we'll find each other and be each other's prize. I release my anger and sadness, emptying my cup so that it's ready to be filled with the peace of mind, joy, and love I deserve.

DAY 12

Dating Mr. PR Agent, Living with Mr. Reality

Living in the past is a dull and lonely business; looking back strains the neck muscles, causes you to bump into people not going your way.

—Edna Ferber

There's no way around it, you're going to be thinking about the heartbreaker, and the broken relationship, for a while. You're going to be hitting your mental rewind button so many times that, with luck, you'll get sick and tired of the nonstop could have/should have/why didn't I? monologue, not to mention the ever-popular, "If I'd been a better girlfriend/mate/partner/whatever, he wouldn't have turned into such a rude, childish, thoughtless, self-centered idiot."

Again, some of that second-guessing and self-blame is inevitable, but please try to get it out of your system as soon as possible. Because every time you let one of those thoughts take up space in your head, no matter how briefly, you're handing your power right back over to your heartbreaker again. For one thing, you probably did quite enough of that while you were in the relationship, right? For another thing, I don't think he could have made it more apparent that he's not qualified to handle it properly. He wasn't even bright enough to appreciate you and make you feel appreciated, after all, and it doesn't get much dumber than that. So now that he's out of your life, you're still going to entrust your God-given power to a man you wouldn't trust to take care of your pet goldfish for a week? Thanks, but I don't think so.

Rather than an official exercise, here's a recommendation for today and for future reference: when you're thinking too much about him, especially when you're in danger of romanticizing him into virtual perfection, I want you to play a game that's been a helpful eye-opener for me and for a whole lot of other women I've worked with over the years: divide him into the two people he probably became and then ask yourself if the memory you're obsessing over was attributable to Mr. PR Agent or to the man who replaced him, Mr. Reality.

Mr. PR Agent is that kind, attentive, generous, playful, enthusiastic, stimulating, goal-oriented man who made you feel like the luckiest woman on earth for the first few weeks or months you were together. (And yes, fair is fair: we women put our best dainty feet forward at first too, it's human nature, but we're talking about him now.) Mr. PR Agent wants to charm you and impress you and win you over, and he gears his efforts toward those goals until he feels secure—and, I'm sorry to say, until he's confident that a vast majority of the time he's going to get his way because, let's face it, our lives run so much more smoothly when our men are content.

Then, sometimes slowly but surely, sometimes almost overnight, Mr. PR Agent's body is mysteriously taken over by the man you're going to be dealing with from now on: Mr. Reality. Sometimes abrupt, sometimes given to endless monologues about subjects he wrongly assumes you're interested in because he is. Ready and eager to correct all your flaws "for your own good," often accompanied by name-calling or colorful adjectives like "stupid" or "selfish" or "fat" or "lazy" or any number of other descriptive outbursts he wouldn't tolerate from you for one second. Given to actual pouting when you don't immediately and automatically cooperate with his agenda (the way you used to). Impatient with your priorities, which he seemed so supportive of not that long ago, if they conflict with his. Mr. PR Agent thought you were fabulous. But somehow, to Mr. Reality, nothing you do is quite good enough, and in general you're just going to be a big old disappointment if you don't shape up—and he'll be the judge of what "shaping up" really means, thanks.

We've all been there. We've all watched friends go there and pulled our hair out wishing they'd wake up. Sadly, we can all name a few women who waited years for that wonderful Mr. PR Agent to come back, when the truth is, Mr. Reality is there to stay, breaking their hearts, their spirits, and sometimes their bank accounts. We say to ourselves, "How do these guys manage to get away with it?" And there's only one honest answer: "Because, thanks to us, they can."

By the way, I'm sure there are some rare women out there for whom Mr. PR Agent and Mr. Reality turned out to be one and the same guy. I'm also sure you join me in giving them a standing ovation. But they're not reading this book, so let's get back to you, and the standing ovation *you* deserve, because you're free, you're moving on, and even though you don't quite believe me yet, this is the beginning of an incredibly exciting time in your life and you don't have to split your attention and your head space for one more minute between yourself and a man who didn't appreciate it anyway.

It's all about you now. You've taken a backseat to him for your own attention quite long enough. It's your turn, and how great is that?

Remember Etch A Sketch toys when we were kids? You'd painstakingly draw a beautiful little picture in the sand inside the frame, and then when you were done enjoying it you'd turn the Etch A Sketch upside down, shake it back and forth, and have a brand-new slate of smooth sand to start another beautiful little picture in, one line at a time. That's a wonderful image for you to focus on right now: your life is a brand-new slate of smooth sand, and you can draw anything on it you want, without anyone looking over your shoulder telling you what you *should* be drawing (or what they drew once that was so much better than what you're drawing), or asking if you're about finished with that stupid drawing so you can pay attention to what they want to do.

*   *   *

And here's a little footnote for the Mr. PR Agent/Mr. Reality game:

My three favorite words in the world are "I love you."

My three second favorite words in the world are "And so what?" When used properly and often, they can really help put things in perspective and remind you that your power belongs to you and nobody else. For example:

Mr. Reality didn't appreciate how special you are? *And so what?* It doesn't mean that you aren't special; it means that he's not, or he would have appreciated you.

You tried your damnedest, but the relationship with Mr. Reality didn't work. *And so what?* It doesn't mean that you don't work, it means that the two of you together don't work, and what a luxury to find that out now, as opposed to five or ten years from now. (I can't resist quoting Dr. Phil again: "The only thing worse than staying in a bad relationship for a year is staying in a bad relationship for a year and one day.")

Mr. Reality left? *And so what?* Who on earth wants someone around who doesn't want to be there? And if he doesn't want to be there, he's a fool. As my girlfriend Lindsay says in situations like that, "Got everything? Watch your head. And don't forget to check the overhead bins."

Mr. Reality's got someone else? *And so what?* So she gets to have *your* old life, as soon as Mr. PR Agent vanishes and Mr. Reality takes over. Lucky her. All the insults, all the withholding, all the blaming, all the whining, all the wet towels on the floor, all the clutter, all the endless monologues about his vast areas of expertise—*zzzzzzz!*—hers, all hers now, bless her heart, while you're off doing exactly what you want to do, exactly when you want to do it. Break out the confetti and let me hear "Amen!"

DAY 13

Get Off the Cross— We Need the Wood

While others may argue about whether the world ends with a bang or a whimper, I just want to make sure mine doesn't end with a whine.

—BARBARA GORDON

Sometimes I think the phrase "owning our power" has been overused, so much so that it's lost its impact.

Let's revive it, because it's such a satisfying, important way to live life.

A quick note before we start, about what owning our power is not: we've all known people who think being powerful means being aggressive and intimidating—in other words, being a bully. I've never known a bully who wasn't a coward, and I've never known a bully who didn't end up alone, miserable, or both. So please, let's just focus on what owning our power *really* means.

Owning our power is discovering how and where we can most effectively, generously, and consistently live up to our greatest physical, mental, emotional, and spiritual potential, and then having the courage and commitment to avoid anyone and anything that tries to dim the light of that potential.

Owning our power is staying fully present in whatever pursuits will lead us to our greatest potential. "Fully present," by the way, is the polar opposite of being preoccupied with what he might be doing or thinking right now, or what he or you said or did that might have been misunderstood, or any form of the what-if trap. You don't have the time, the energy, or the patience for preoccupation anymore. You're busy minding your own business. You're busy tending to your own growth. You're busy building an authentic life, unapologetic about who you are and what you want, embracing those who want to soar right along with you, and saying "No, thank you" to those who can only feel comfortable about themselves by keeping you close to the ground. You're busy learning that you don't have to *try* to be anymore—you can just be. You're busy discovering all there is to know about the most important person in your life, the love of your life, in fact—you. You're busy, in other words, reclaiming and owning your power, and when you do, mark my words, you'll never give it away again.

Today's Exercise

I want you to sit down with your journal/diary/workbook and write the words "I am" at the top of the page.

Now, I want you to list all the adjectives you would love to overhear others apply to you, and that you would love to *honestly* be able to use to describe yourself:

Thoughtful

Loving

Kind

Generous

Smart

Fair

Hard-working

Reliable

Honest

Courageous

Inspiring

Disciplined

Open-minded

And so on. Put a lot of thought into each entry on your list, so that as you write it, you can spend a moment imagining how much better your life will be, and what thoughtful, loving, kind, generous, etc., people you'll attract, as you work on enhancing each of those attributes that are already part of your potential.

Last but not least, under each entry, write down one thing you can do, no matter how small or how much of a baby step, to make that adjective more of a reality in your life. Then put each of those baby steps on your to-do list for tomorrow.

Every time you accomplish a baby step, write down a new one for your next to-do list.

Keep it up throughout the remainder of your thirty-day heartbreak cure, and guess what: coming closer and closer every day to every attribute you're yearning for will become such a habit that you won't have to write it down or even think about it anymore. You'll just do it. And one morning you'll wake up knowing you truly deserve every adjective on that list, and that only a truly powerful woman could have made it happen.

Today's Affirmation

As of this moment . . .
I am reclaiming my heart.
I am reclaiming my mind.
I am reclaiming my time.
And above all, I am reclaiming my kindest, most generous, most useful power.
I will never forfeit it again. I have myself back.
I am free.
I am whole.
I am.

And now, in case you've been forgetting, make sure you've drawn that X you've earned through every day, including Day 13, on your calendar. I hope you're as proud of yourself as I am of you.

DAY 14

Bitter Party of One, Your Table Is Waiting

Our real blessings often appear to us in the shape of pains, losses, and disappointments.

—Joseph Addison

I once worked with a lovely young actress who met a man and promptly entered into a committed relationship with him. He moved to New York and into her apartment, and for a while she almost seemed to be getting more beautiful by the day.

But within six months, her face began to change. She started looking brittle, older, pinched, and tired, to the point where I was privately wondering if she might be ill. As anyone who knows me well will tell you, I'm available as can be if you want to talk, but I'll never pry. So I would simply ask her how she was doing, to which this once happy, enthusiastic woman would reply with a stream of negativity and complaints about everything from her dressing room to her hair stylist to her scenes for that day to the weather to, almost, the color of the sky. There was no steering her into a positive conversation no matter how hard I tried, and I sadly gave up and started avoiding her whenever possible.

This went on for three years—*three years!*—until one day we cast members all returned from a long holiday break, and what do you know, that beautiful, radiant woman I hadn't seen in so long came waltzing happily back to work. She looked ten years younger. Rested. Relaxed. Peaceful. I was probably staring at her because she quickly walked over and engaged me in conversation, and guess what: she was a complete delight again, positive and funny and fun and full of enthusiasm.

I asked her as casually as possible how her holidays were and what was new in her life (resisting the temptation to ask, "What the hell happened to you?!"), and she replied simply, "I broke up with my fiancé."

My first reaction was shock. My second reaction, the blink of an eye later, was, "Duh." I hadn't been consciously aware that they'd been having problems, but I'd worn that same pinched, brittle, tired, older-than-my-years face before, and I couldn't believe I hadn't seen enough of myself in her to figure out what was happening. The more she opened up about it, the more I felt as if I really was looking into a mirror of my own past. She'd been terribly unhappy for two-thirds of the relationship without wanting to admit it, even to herself. She believed him when he berated her and tried everything she could think of, and everything that he demanded, to be a better girlfriend. The harder she tried, the less he seemed to respect her, at the expense of her self-confidence. She dreaded being home with him, but work was no fun either, as her belief in herself and her talent eroded. A dynamic had evolved between the two of them in which she just plain couldn't win. And let's face it, there's only one response to finding yourself in a game you can't win: *stop playing!* Finally she caught on to that option, and out he went.

I've thought of her ever since as a lovely, perfect example of a fact we tend to forget when we're not paying attention: we women really do wear our lives on our faces. I don't care how much makeup we're wearing or how brilliantly it's applied. If we're happy, at peace, and confident, we're beautiful. Each and every one of us. But if we're an emotional mess? We can't seem to get it straight that no, showing all our teeth doesn't actually trick people into thinking we're smiling, and even the most exquisite eyes lose some of their beauty when there's no light coming from them.

Obviously, the solution is to simply be happy all the time from now on. If that somehow doesn't work out (*you think?!*), there really are some helpful things to keep in mind at this time in your life when you're probably carrying, and wearing, a whole lot of pain, sadness, anger, and resentment.

I want you to take a long, hard look at the possibility that you're struggling with the breakup much more than you're struggling with the loss of a relationship that by definition was too flawed, for whatever reasons, to continue. After all, the goal is supposed to be the polar opposite of what my coworker went through: physically and emotionally thriving *in* the relationship, not when we've finally found our way to the exit one way or another. Look back. Can you honestly say you were thriving with your heartbreaker (aside from unavoidable factors like illnesses, menopause, and so forth)? Were you at your physical and emotional best? Or is a lot of the pain, sadness, anger, and resentment you're feeling now a whole lot of residual unexpressed emotion you held back during the relationship in an effort to prove to him, yourself, and the rest of the world what a happy, perfect girlfriend you were—or because he hated it when you "whined and complained" so you kept quiet to keep peace? If the honest answer is that it's the life-changing fact of the relationship ending that's upsetting you, rather than the loss of the relationship itself, there's great news: somewhere in that jumble of emotions you're going to find relief, celebration, and peace of mind just waiting for you to let them emerge.

Anger is energy. It's its own force field. If you ever doubt that, walk into a room where a truly angry person is sitting. I don't care if they don't say a word or give you a single visible hint that they're in a rage. I'm betting you'll instantly feel uncomfortable, no matter how happy you might have been just moments earlier. You'll have the urge to walk right back out again. I felt it around my coworker at the time without taking the time to identify it, I've felt it around angry friends and total strangers now that I'm conscious of it, and I'm sure people felt it around me before I became more adept at the healthy, appropriate, disciplined releasing of that very viable energy.

So, yes. Venting is essential, even good for the complexion. *But only if it's healthy, appropriate, and disciplined!* And here are some clear-cut guidelines to provide you with maximum venting benefit and minimum venting damage:

Strictly Off-Limits Venting

1. The heartbreaker, his friends, his family, and his coworkers. I know. You want him, or at least someone close to him, to really understand what he did to you, and—theoretically, I guess—say or do something to make you feel better. But in addition to the fact that the odds against that are somewhere between slim and none, and that historically those conversations are doomed to fail thanks to heightened emotions, tempers, egos, and blame, there's one inarguable truth at the core of all this turbulence: he has no place in your life anymore. He is history. You're moving on. He is none of your business, and, more significantly, *you are none of his business*. I promise, the sooner you get in the habit of recognizing that and behaving accordingly (even if it takes you a while to believe it), the sooner you'll start feeling *so* much better!

2. Coworkers, acquaintances, and strangers. Tempting as it might be to take it out on anyone and everyone who happens to be in your convenient proximity, you can count on it that (a) it won't make you feel one bit better, and (b) you'll create a whole lot of negativity for a

whole lot of innocent bystanders who don't need it and have enough problems of their own. In fact, not only do I want you not to vent with these people, I want you to go out of your way to be kind to them. Make a little extra effort to help that coworker. Pay a compliment to that acquaintance. Ask that waiter, or salesperson, or cashier how *they* are. Not only will you feel better about yourself with each kindness and get your mind off yourself for a moment or two, but you'll also notice that kindness is every bit as contagious as anger, so you'll be helping to create a much more pleasant, relaxing atmosphere for yourself when you need it most.

Strictly *On*-Limits Venting

1. I'm a big fan of therapists. If you already have one, take full advantage of him or her, and vent your heart out. If you don't already have one and can find an affordable one through a reliable referral, I think you'll truly benefit from the experience. For the price of admission you can vent your heart out, with well-educated guidance and feedback, and not once will you ever have to be polite and ask your therapist how *he* is.

2. On the other hand, if therapy isn't among your options for whatever reason, ask your most trusted, discreet, nonjudgmental friend or two (at most—we don't want this to become a full-time hobby) for three one-hour venting sessions per week, when you can say anything

and everything you're feeling whether you mean it or not, as impolitely as you might feel like saying it. Two conditions, though, and make them hold you to it: only one hour at a time, and for every hour they devote to listening patiently to you, they get ten minutes for you to listen to them, how they are, and what's happening in their lives. You're allowed some self-indulgence right now, but total self-absorption is never okay, particularly when it comes to great friends.

3. We'll call this Letters He'll Never Read: I want you to open your journal/diary/workbook to the next blank page and start writing your heartbreaker a letter, or letters, in which you absolutely spill your guts. Say every wonderful or horrible thing that's been floating around in your head and in the pit of your stomach. Uncensored. Unapologetic. Probably best of all, un-encumbered by all those excuses and defenses and confusing sidetracks you'd have to try to slog your way through if you were trying to say all this to him in person. After an opening "Dear (his name, or impolite nickname)," tell him how and why he's made you so sad and so furious and so confused; remind him of the stupid, outrageous things he did and said; point out every generous thing you did for him that he never bothered to reciprocate; critique his rude, obnoxious, thoughtless, bossy, mean, selfish, juvenile behavior. Hold nothing back, just let 'er rip, for as long as you like and as many pages as it takes.

And then, here's the most important part: DON'T EVER, *EVER* LET HIM SEE THOSE PAGES! They're for your eyes and your benefit only, and it's a 100 percent guarantee that no good will come from his reading them. You'll regret it for years, believe me, and don't forget, you can never take back those hyperemotional venting words, any more than you can unring a bell.

Instead, so that you really can have the satisfaction of mailing your Letters He'll Never Read, I'm completely serious, I want you to seal them in an envelope without your name, put a stamp on them, and send them to:

Catherine Hickland
P.O. Box 290
North Hollywood, CA 91603

I will never open them; you have my word. They're none of my business, and, again, they're purely for your benefit, not mine. I will simply see to it that they're thoroughly and completely destroyed. Send as many as you want as often as you want until you've said everything you want to say to your heartbreaker—or, better yet, until you're just not interested enough or too busy to write them anymore.

Oh, and just a couple more things for today: draw a nice big *X* on Day 14 of your calendar and spend a quiet moment of gratitude for how far you've come in these two weeks and what great work you've done to earn all that progress.

And don't forget . . .

Today's Affirmation

I am worth so much more than what I've just been through, and I'm taking every step to see to it that I'll never go through it again. Just being safe and strong enough to fearlessly express myself is proof that I'm free, that life is getting more beautiful by the minute, and that I'm more ready with each passing day for peace, joy, and miracles.

DAY 15

It's Not What You're Eating, It's What's Eating You

I have found that if you love life, life will love you back.

—ARTHUR RUBENSTEIN

Weight. I can't think of a subject that creates more of an instant bond between women everywhere. We talk about it constantly. We swap diet and medication tips. We tell war stories. We share celebrations of weight losses—sometimes, inexplicably, with pizza and ice cream. We share tears and frustrations when our skinny jeans stop fitting, and we agonize over the indignity of shopping for bathing suits. Or, just as horribly, we have friends and family begging us to gain a few pounds as we try to deny that we're wasting away.

Yes, I speak fluent weight. I've struggled with my weight all my life. I've been so sadly overweight I wanted to hide, and I've been so underweight that I bordered on anorexia. So with the exception of that handful of you who have the bodies you want and don't give it a thought, whichever way your scales have tipped beyond your health and comfort levels, I've been there, I understand, and I especially want to focus on this important issue at this time in your life when you're heartbroken, vulnerable, unsteady on your feet, and in danger of exaggerating your least self-loving behavior.

You've probably read this a thousand times, and it's just plain true for the most part: everything that happens from the neck down is the result of what's happening from the neck up. Or, to put it another equally effective way, it's not what you eat, but why you eat. And yes, there are absolutely exceptions to that. Weight can also be affected by everything from thyroid or adrenal or other physiological irregularities to menopause (take it from me) to certain prescription medications. Which is why I would love for you to run, not walk, to your doctor, if it's physically and financially possible, and get a complete physical unless you've had one in the past six months. (I know. I don't enjoy it either, but we're insane to pretend we have better things to do.) Tackling weight issues is tough enough without our bodies quietly sabotaging every step we take, and in an ideal world, we women would be as well informed about what's up with *us* as we are about every diet and diet pill on the market.

Of course, a vast majority of the time, whether we're overeating to fill and comfort a void in our hearts and souls or undereating to starve and punish that same void, our bodies are a direct reflection of our emotional health. And during a time of heartbreak, our emotional health is guaranteed to be compromised. In addition to sadness, depression, confusion, and anger, we're especially vulnerable to one of the most insidious killers of all: stress. Make no mistake—stress is a killer. When it's not weakening our immune systems, wreaking havoc on our blood pressure, causing ulcers, and planting seeds for any number of aches, pains, and diseases, it's busy killing our joy, self-esteem, and ability to concentrate. As far as our eating habits go, stress typically makes us either eat as if it's our last meal on earth or starve ourselves into oblivion. If you've found yourself falling victim to one of those patterns since your heartbreak, put a lot of the blame on the understandable stress you're feeling, remind yourself that the more you give in to bad health habits the more stress you're adding to your life, and, above all, make up your mind that right now, right this minute, you're going to stop punishing yourself and start loving yourself again. Needless to say, you're worth loving at any weight, but when you truly love yourself as much as you deserve, you won't tolerate taking anything less than the best possible care of yourself.

I'm not about to even pretend that in these few pages I can tell you things about weight management that you haven't already heard. I can tell you that diets don't work, but you know that. If they did, there wouldn't be thousands of them coming along, and fading away, every ten minutes. I can tell you that exercise is essential, but you know that too, and as someone who doesn't exactly leap out of bed in the morning yelling, "Yippee! Gym day!" I hear many of you groaning at the mere mention of exercise in a way that's eerily familiar to me. I can tell you that no matter how effective they might be temporarily, your body's going to pay the price for diet pills the minute you stop taking them, and none of them are designed to be taken for the rest of your life.

What I will urge you to do as of today's exercise (pardon the expression) if you have any weight issues at all—after that complete physical, of course—is go online, research, and find and commit to, not a diet, but a *plan* that offers you enough of a healthy variety of foods you enjoy that you can adopt it as a way of life. Ideally, the plan won't just limit you to a narrow list of options or a specific brand of frozen foods. It will educate you on how to eat well and healthfully in any situation and lifestyle from today on, so that what you eat and don't eat isn't about discipline and deprivation anymore, it's actually about preference.

I'm a fan of Weight Watchers for that reason because it educates while it works, and it's a lifestyle option rather than something you stop doing when you've reached your ideal weight or size. There's a lot of great information about it online, including online weigh-ins for those who don't have the time or desire to attend meetings in person. I've also found food combining to be effective, luxuriously versatile, and just plain sensible. Suzanne Somers has written several very smart books on the subject of food combining, and a book called *Fit for Life* by Harvey and Marilyn Diamond walks you through it beautifully as well. Dr. Phil's *Ultimate Weight Solution: The 7 Keys to Weight Loss Freedom* is an excellent, practical, educational resource too.

As for exercise, let's face it, that can be almost more of a nightmare issue than food. I feel safe in saying that if we haven't personally fallen for almost every trick in the book, we've got friends who have. I've lost count of the number of gyms I've joined and then wandered away from after a few weeks or months. I have friends who took up jogging, power walking, and running with the greatest enthusiasm, only to admit once they've quit that they actually hated it but hoped they'd learn to like it. And let's not even discuss the money we've all invested in "can't miss" home exercise equipment that it turns out we can ignore quite easily, thanks, no matter where we put it.

The real issue about exercise is that we feel better, and our bodies thank us, when we *move*, and if we think long and hard enough, there's something we can enjoy doing on a regular basis that involves momement. It can range from gardening to walking dogs to yoga to dance lessons to karate to Pilates classes to painting the living room to golf to horseback riding to—pretty much you name it. All I ask is that you combine the concepts of "movement" and "love it" and you'll find something to do often enough to make it a pleasurable habit, not a chore.

What I most want to impress upon you today is the following:

In case you've forgotten, or it's just been a while, experience how great it feels to feel great.

Be proud every single day of how terrific you look—not for anyone else, but for yourself.

Don't spend one more moment feeling out of control, or helpless, about whatever improvements you want to make in your body, your weight, your health choices. This day, this minute, you're going to start loving yourself enough to take charge, find the plans that fit you and your life, and never, ever think about dieting again.

Remember that right now you need to take even better care of yourself than usual, while you're healing and recovering.

And maybe most of all, erase every past weight management failure from your mind. You're not who you were then. You're not even who you were yesterday. You didn't know then what you know now. You're an exciting, evolving, utterly unique, and thrilling work in progress, and no one—not even you—will ever again stand between you and your greatest potential that still lies ahead of you.

Today's Affirmation

Today I choose to love myself, and reflect it through my eating and general health habits. My days of looking and feeling less than my best are behind me, as I commit to a new lifestyle rather than to a diet. In the process of starting my new lifestyle plan I'm also learning that I really am reclaiming my power, and I'm excited and very proud of myself.

DAY 16

Your Higher Power: You Are Not Alone

We deserve preferential treatment not because of who we are, but because of whose we are.

—Joel Osteen

My childhood home in Florida was a lovely house with a pretty Spanish tiled roof at the corner of Dysfunction Boulevard and Chaos Street. I'm the youngest of three children, and even before I came along my family was in complete emotional turmoil. It was unsafe in my house, out of control, with adults who were far too caught up in their own self-destruction to focus on the needs of a child.

I knew instinctively that I was too young and too little to change things, so I busied my tiny self acting as if everything was okay, being a caretaker and secret-keeper for the grown-ups and cleaning up other people's messes (literally and figuratively). I scrambled to the relative safety of survivor behavior and held on tight—too tight, as it turned out, since I continued clinging to it as an adult and it hurt me terribly.

By the time I was six I was pretty much on my own emotionally, and I apparently knew it, because I began manifesting, spontaneously and unconsciously. The good news is, I became incredibly self-sufficient at a very early age. The bad news is, I ended up creating all sorts of chaos in my adult life because, to put it simply, according to my first and most powerful adult role models, I thought we were supposed to.

My one beam of light from the world of grown-ups emanated from my grandmother. I called her Gram. Gram was a farm woman who made up for her lack of formal education with a whole world of common sense. She was hilarious without knowing it, frank and honest and agenda-free, and the generosity of her love when things got really bad at home was my lifeline. I adored her, and I admired her, and even now, all these decades later, I miss her every day.

For as long as I could remember I'd been mesmerized by a glorious building with a massive stained glass facade a few miles from Gram's house. I stared at it every time we drove by, and I longed to go inside, not just to see it but because it looked, to this child's eyes, as if there was comfort to be found there. I had never heard my parents or Gram speak a word about religion or spirituality—my mother was a lapsed Catholic and my father was a nonbeliever—but this building, which Gram told me was a Presbyterian church, struck me from the first time I saw it as a place God might live.

And so one day when I was eight years old I asked Gram

if she would please drop me off at that magnificent building when Sunday services were going on. To this day I have no idea where that fire in my heart, that urgent yearning, came from to have the honor of being welcomed into God's house, but I knew I had to be there, and I'll always believe it was divine intervention in the life of a lost little girl.

The following Sunday, and every Sunday after that for a very long time, my beloved Gram would drop me off in front of the Presbyterian church in her giant old red Cadillac that looked like the Batmobile. I'd proudly and confidently make my way to the front pew so that I could hear every word the silver-haired minister had to say, and so that he could see me and duly count me among the reverent.

I'll always wonder who he thought that tiny girl in the front pew belonged to, but he never asked. At the end of every service, he would descend from the pulpit, walk past me, and give me a fatherly wink and a smile before heading through the congregation to the grand front doors, where he would shake hands with each congregant as they left the church. I couldn't wait to shake his hand every Sunday. He was, after all, a celebrity of the highest order—he knew God *personally*!

I lived for that hour in that church every week, where somebody not only noticed me but told me in the most beautiful, comforting words that God loved me, protected me, was with me every moment, and would share every burden if I would only let him. I've always believed that the soul knows the truth when it hears it, and even as an eight-year-old, I knew that was the truth. I knew God had summoned me into his magnificent house when it became apparent that no one around me was going to tell me about him, and he wasn't about to let me live one more day without him.

Or, to put it another way, God called and I answered. The only times I find myself in serious trouble are when I hang up on him, either because I get so busy being busy or because I let fear and self-doubt eclipse the single most important truth in my life: I am never alone!

And I promise, my cherished friend, neither are you.

Not for a moment am I dismissing any belief system that's different from mine. You're absolutely entitled to believe that you have to do everything all by yourself. I'm just here to assure you that you don't have to, especially right now when your heart is broken. God, who created you and adores you as his own, is waiting to take you into his sacred arms and dissolve your pain with his perfect, unconditional love.

Please, whatever else you believe, believe this: you have the power to put your heartbreak into God's hands and let it go.

Being God's creation, you are divine, and the divine *never* settle, or wish themselves back with someone who made them feel less than who they are and *whose* they are.

Settling for less is the death of joy, and a form of turning your back on God, who will never, ever turn his back on you.

Together you and God will heal your heart so that it's even stronger and wiser than it was before, and the day will come when you'll thank him for all you learned from this heartbreak with his guidance.

Because of the constant presence of your Creator, there never has been and never will be a single moment when you are not loved.

Today: A Prayer

Heavenly Father,

Sometimes, especially in times of pain, I need to be reminded of things I already know. And what I know is that you're here with me right now, loving me, healing my heart, promising to help me always cherish my worth as a child of yours and never let anyone make me feel diminished again. May this pain inform me rather than weaken me. May I embrace it as a result of my own choices, each one of which is an opportunity to learn and grow closer to your dreams for me, which far exceed my own.

You know my heart far better than I, and I commit it to you, with all my faith and trust, that you'll fill it in good time with the kind, true, respectful love a child of yours deserves and nothing less. I pray for guidance toward living every day in devoted service to your greatest, most compassionate good. Amen.

DAY 17

It Isn't "Out There"

*Knowing others is wisdom; knowing yourself
is enlightenment.*

—LAO TZU

First and foremost, have I mentioned recently enough that
you're doing *great*, and I'm so proud of you?

I hope this thirty-day journey we're taking together is
starting to offer glimmers of the fact that heartbreak can
be an excellent teacher and an excellent motivator. I hope
you're appreciating, if only a little, how much you've grown
and evolved since Day 1, thanks to your own hard work
and—yes, I'll say it—thanks to the end of a relationship
that you obviously chose for that very reason. It's a simple
fact that we sometimes only see clearly in hindsight: some
relationships have to end in order for us to evolve. When
we're back in our right minds, and those oppressive dark
clouds of grief are lifting, we become willing and available
to learn all the lessons we can from the experience, and

someday, I promise you, you'll be grateful for your hard-won wisdom.

In the meantime, just look forward to the fact that the other side of this turmoil is where the light is. Where the sanity is. Where the contentment is. Where the fun is. On the other side of this turmoil is the awareness that, whether you ended the relationship or he did, what felt like the worst day of your life just a couple of weeks ago has the potential to be the *best* day of your life. Why? Because it's made you available to focus your attention on a relationship that's infinitely more important than the one you just left behind. In fact, it's the most important relationship you'll ever have in this lifetime: your relationship with yourself.

I want you to write this down in your journal/diary/workbook and read it as many times as it takes for you to "make it yours" and believe it:

No other relationship you will ever experience can offer as much potential security, comfort, safety, and peace of mind as your relationship with yourself. Learn to be self-sufficient and to love your own company and watch how effortlessly you attract other people.

It honestly makes the hair on the back of my neck stand up when a woman refers to a new love in her life by saying he "completes" her, or that he feels like "the other half of her." Romantic as that might sound if we're not paying attention, it's also nonsense. Just as we are, we are not incomplete. We are not a bunch of half-people walking around. We are whole, valuable, and quite enough all by ourselves. We *are* enough. We *have* enough. Everything we need is already within us. Yes, other people can add a lot of joy and love to our lives. But if we take the time to find the joy and love we already possess, we'll stop holding ourselves hostage to the myth that we have to depend on someone else to provide it, and often choose that someone else too quickly or for the wrong reasons.

I've also seen, and so have you, women who stayed in downright horrifying relationships, even compromising their own safety and the safety of their children, because "I don't want to be alone." I never doubt for a moment that someday, if and when they summon the power and courage to say enough is enough, they'll look back and realize something I learned the hard way myself: I was never lonelier than when I was hanging on to a doomed relationship. "Alone" is not a dirty word. It's not a curse. It can be as rich and fulfilling as you allow it to be when you stop looking "out there" and start looking "in here."

"In here" is the one person you're guaranteed to be with every single day for the rest of your life, no matter what, no matter who else comes and goes.

"In here" is the only person you can ever change.

"In here" is the only person who can see to it that you reach your greatest potential.

"In here" is the only person who's always interested in what you have to say, the only person who'll always get every single one of your jokes, the only person you'll never have to do battle with over the remote control, the only person who always wants exactly the same thing you do for dinner exactly when you're hungry.

"In here" is your power.

"In here" is your hope.

"In here" is your strength.

"In here" is your faith.

"In here" is your truth.

"In here" are all the answers.

"In here" is the vigilant guardian of your dignity, your integrity, your kindness, and your emotional security.

"In here" is the one-of-a-kind person you were born to be and born to become.

"In here" is a world of love.

"In here," in other words, is a magnificent place to live and explore.

And that's what I want you to do today, and tomorrow, and for as long as it takes for you to feel completely whole and content and cherished "in here." Because once you accomplish that, it's a fairly safe bet that you'll love "in here" far too much to ever let anyone disrespect, dishonor, or dismiss it again.

Love who you are.

Love who you're becoming.

You are enough, all by yourself.

You always were.

You always will be.

Sleep well.

Today's Affirmation

I know that when I truly love and honor myself, I am at my best and most complete, and I will never settle for anything less from myself or from anyone else, ever again.

DAY 18

Giving It Up

Holding resentment is like eating poison and
then waiting for the other person to keel over.

—Anonymous

I want the life that lies ahead for you to be greater than you can possibly imagine. I want it to be full of peace and kindness and emotional prosperity and love that amazes you with its depth and simplicity.

Today we're going to talk about an essential step toward that life.

We're going to talk about forgiving your heartbreaker.

Not forgetting. If you forget, you'll lose the lessons.

Forgiving.

Not for him.

For you.

I have a friend who spent twenty-three years married to a really bad guy. He chronically cheated, lied, stole from her, disappeared for days at a time, had a gambling addiction, and, and, and. (And we've come far enough in these two-plus weeks together to wonder why she wasn't out of there in twenty-three *days*, haven't we?) Finally she packed up their two teenage children and left him.

I learned pretty early on in our friendship that we would never get through an evening together without her launching into yet another tirade about Truman, usually including several anecdotes, like the night she woke up to find him stealing money from her purse, or the day she walked into his office to find him in a highly compromising position with one of her closest friends. While telling these stories her voice would raise to almost a shout, her face would flush with anger, the veins in her neck would tighten, and she'd be as livid as if every incident she was obsessing about had happened just last week.

Here's the but: their divorce had been final for eighteen years, and they'd rarely spoken since.

One night at dinner, I admit it, I just couldn't sit through one more Truman rant, so when she started into yet another story I interrupted and said, "I have to ask you a question. Have you spent one moment in the past eighteen years celebrating the fact that you're not married to that awful man anymore?"

She stared at me for a long time, looking absolutely shocked, before she answered, "No. I haven't. I can't believe it, but I've been so busy hating him that I forgot to celebrate!"

The translation, of course, is that in forgetting to celebrate, she "forgot" to let him go, to forgive him, to move him out of her life once and for all. She "forgot" to appreciate that for eighteen years she'd been a single, successful, talented, attractive woman with beautiful children and grandchildren. And no one paid the price for that but her. He'd long since remarried and moved to Europe, so he certainly wasn't suffering from her inability to forgive him. But she was the first to admit, the more we talked about it, that she'd devoted so much time and energy to the bitterness, resentment, and rage she felt toward him, she might as well have still been living with him because he was as much a part of her present tense as her morning cup of coffee and her glass of wine with dinner.

To this day, when, purely out of habit, she tries to start a Truman story, all any of us have to do is interrupt her with a simple "Celebrate," and she stops, smiles, and changes the subject.

One of the most common areas of confusion on the subject of forgiveness is the idea that by forgiving we're essentially saying, "That awful thing you did to me was really okay after all." And nothing could be further from the truth. Nothing awful anyone does to us is ever okay. But we only prolong the act itself, and the hurt from it, if we hang on to it and refuse to let it go, like a dog with a brand-new bone.

Another easily confused issue about forgiveness is that somehow, by refusing to forgive a heartbreaker, we're successfully punishing him. Again, that's simply not true.

Just like my friend's ex-husband, who was cozy and happy

with his new wife in Europe, the heartbreaker will have his own karma to deal with in its own good time without our having to lift a finger. (Don't ever doubt the reality of karma, by the way. It's not a theory, it's a universal law.) In the meantime, my friend was living proof that a heart full of resentment, bitterness, and rage actually changes who you are. All that darkness in her soul left a diminished amount of space for light, and children, and grandchildren, and friends, so that, in a way, part of her was inaccessible to those who deserved it most until she released it and remembered to celebrate.

I have no way of proving this, by the way, but considering all the studies that have been done on the physical effect of clinging to any form of negativity, I wouldn't be surprised if my friend's subsequent lumpectomy (benign, thank God) could have been avoided if, years ago, she'd chosen to just forgive, let go, and move on.

There's a wonderful book called *The Language of Letting Go* by Melody Beattie, which describes letting go as learning to calmly let things be. "Letting go," she says, "takes the emotional charge, the drama, out of things and restores us to a sense of balance, peace, and spiritual power. Letting go works well on the past and the future. It brings us into today."

Which is all you and I have to concern ourselves with at the moment, my friend. Today. Our eighteenth day together, and you're doing such great work. If you haven't been keeping up-to-date on putting Xs through the days on your calendar to mark your progress, please remember to do so the minute you're finished reading, because you've earned every one of those marks.

But for now, all I want you to do is sit for a few quiet moments taking long, deep breaths, just letting go. Not forgetting. Simply forgiving. Not for him. For you. And for those who deserve all your attention and all your heart.

Let go.

I promise you won't fall.

All is well.

Today's Exercise

On your bathroom mirror, your refrigerator, inside your front door, or wherever you'll be sure to see it several times a day, please just tape the word "celebrate." You don't need to explain to anyone else what it means unless you want to, but do pay attention to the fact that the more often you see it, the sooner it will begin to make you smile.

Today's Affirmation

Today, maybe for the first time, I experience forgiveness not as a weakness, but as a strength. Forgiving and letting go will make me truly free to live my life and let others live theirs. The life that waits for me is a great one, and I refuse to let another moment of resentment stand in my own way.

DAY 19

When in Doubt,
Believe the Behavior

Actions speak louder than words.

—Everyone from the

first caveman on

I admit it. I don't think the old adage "Actions speak louder than words" has ever had the slightest impact on me, or even registered as something worth paying attention to, in the eleven kazillion times I've heard it in the last fifty-two years. But reworded into "When there's a difference between what they say and how they behave, *believe the behavior!*" it's very valuable advice that we women seem to have an awfully hard time following when it comes to relationships.

I should repeat the key phrase in that sentence: "when it comes to relationships." In general, we can be the brightest, savviest people on earth, able to leap tall buildings in a single bound and spot a con artist a mile away. Let us be in love, though, and have our hearts set on believing what we want to believe, and we're suddenly so confused by any difference between words and behavior that it's a wonder we can find our way to and from work.

Let's say I walk up to you with my very blond hair and say, "Hi, I'm Cat, and I have jet-black hair." I'm betting that you're going to think one of three things: I'm crazy, I'm a pathological liar, or I'm insulting your intelligence. What you're *not* going to think, despite what you're standing there looking at with your own eyes, is "*I* wouldn't say I have jet-black hair if it weren't true, so *you* must be mistaken."

But time and time again, when we're "in love," we'll essentially try to convince ourselves that blond hair is jet black because he says so. The sooner we break that habit the less confused we'll be both during and after the relationships. The good news is, it really is a habit, and it's much easier to figure out than we insist on making it. In fact, believing the behavior, not the words, is a breeze when we see it on paper and we're using our heads rather than our hearts.

Here's a quick little quiz I think you'll pass with flying colors:

- He routinely calls you demeaning, insulting names, ignores you, and embarrasses you in front of your friends. But when you call him on it, he's almost hurt that you would accuse him of disrespecting you because, for your information, he respects you very much. Does he really respect you? Yes or no.
- You catch him in a blatant, hands-down lie. You con-

front him about it and he swears he would never lie to you. Is he a liar? Yes or no.

- He has a disastrous credit rating, he owes hundreds of dollars in unpaid parking tickets, and he's a year behind in child support. He asks to borrow money so that he can pay off his debts and stay out of jail, and he assures you that he'll pay you back because, after all, he loves you too much to rip you off. If you loan him that money, are you likely to ever see it again? Yes or no.

- He tells you when you start dating that he's available. But he finds excuses not to give you his home phone number, you're never invited to his place, you've never met his friends, he never spends the night, and he has to "work" on most major holidays. Is he really available? Yes or no.

  And part 2 of that question: Is he a good candidate for a relationship if he does become available, since he's already established that he's a liar and a cheater by dating you? Yes or no.

See what I mean? They're not confusing at all on paper, are they? They're also great practice for past and future reference. Getting in the habit of believing the behavior when it conflicts with the words can save us (and I do mean *us*) more time, money, and heartache than we can imagine if we just pay attention—and then, of equal importance, make sure our behavior is as consistent with our words as we're going to expect from the future men in our lives. I'm sure at some point or other in our lives we've all proclaimed, "I would never put up with a man who (fill in supposedly unacceptable behavior)," and then looked up to find ourselves with some version of that very man, making excuses and justifying our choices every step of the way. One of the most worthwhile goals we can set is to expect every bit as much consistency between our own words and behavior as we're going to expect from the men in our lives from now on. It comes down to "Say what you mean, and mean what you say." Wouldn't relationships be so much easier if we simply lived by and demanded that, nothing more, nothing less?

And if you need inspiration to help you along if your resolve starts to weaken, remember this story of a friend of mine who recently became my hero.

Her eleven-year marriage to an alcoholic had ended, and when she started dating again two years later she made it very clear to every man she saw more than a couple of times that if he was interested in substance abuse, she'd be moving along, thanks.

Along came a man she found herself really falling for, a man who promised her that alcohol and drugs weren't a part of his life. They'd been seeing each other for a few months, and it certainly seemed that he'd told her the truth, until one night she was looking through his kitchen drawers for a cooking utensil and came across a vial of cocaine. She was devastated and immediately confronted him with it. His explanation: it wasn't his, it belonged to his roommate, who was conveniently out of the country and couldn't be reached to confirm or deny the story.

My friend spent a couple of days agonizing over whether or not to believe him before she got tired of agonizing and decided to find out one way or the other before she invested another moment in this man. The next night over dinner she presented him with a drug test. If he chose to take it and passed, great. If he refused, for whatever reason, she had no intention of ever seeing him again, or even staying long enough to finish dinner.

He took the test without a moment of hesitation, and he passed with flying colors. (I know. I honestly didn't see that coming either.) They've been together almost five years now, and I'm not sure I've ever seen two people who respect each other more—she witnessed early on the consistency between his words and his behavior, and he learned early on that she says what she means and she means what she says.

A great lesson for all of us, don't you think? Which leads very neatly to . . .

Today's Exercise

Don't spend more than half an hour at most on this first part: I want you to take out your journal/diary/workbook and start writing examples of those times when your heartbreaker's words were at odds with his behavior and you chose to do yourself a disservice by believing his words. Not for a moment are you allowed to beat yourself up about it. You're just putting it on paper so you can look at it, examine how and why it happened, and learn how to prevent it from happening again in your future relationships. Remember, the only mistakes we should have trouble forgiving ourselves for are the ones we don't learn from and keep repeating.

The second part of this exercise is ongoing, and you can start first thing tomorrow. All I want you to do is start really paying attention to the consistencies and inconsistencies between words and actions in the people around you. Write them down if you can or need to, whatever it takes to make that observation a habit, and then act according to what you learn.

It's my hope and belief that by the time your next potential relationship comes along, you won't be fooled again, or contribute your own inconsistencies, when the words don't match the behavior.

Today's Affirmation

Today and from this day forward I'm excited to anticipate the integrity, clarity, and peace of mind in my life that will come from learning and perfecting the skill of demanding and offering reliable consistency between words and behavior, and accepting that when that consistency is absent, the truth is in the behavior.

DAY 20

The Inventory

Do. Or do not. There is no try.

—YODA

We can't change anyone but ourselves.

That's not a theory. It's a fact.

Ninety-nine women out of a hundred know that.

Almost none of us believe it.

I swear, if we women could get over this habit of looking at our potential love interests as piles of modeling clay we can change, fix, transform, whip into shape, we'd be so much better off, and, frankly, so would a lot of the men in our lives. How utterly careless and irresponsible of us that we often put more thought into buying a car or even choosing a new brand of makeup than we put into selecting someone we'll be inviting into our homes and our beds.

This is a whole other issue than the difference between the early best-behavior Mr. PR Agent phase and the inevitable arrival of Mr. Reality. This is about the fact that we often learn volumes of vitally important details about a man before we get involved, but then, rather than assessing how we feel about those details and whether or not they're okay with us, we either find euphemisms for the ones we don't like, excuse them away with a battery of tired clichés, or scoff at them because they'll be such a breeze to fix once we get a good foothold in his life.

The euphemisms sound something like this, by the way: if he's moody and volatile and we're determined to overlook it, we call him "complicated"; if he's an unreliable flake who can't hold a job, he's "still finding himself"; and so forth.

The tired clichés? We either loaned him bail money or fell for a convicted felon because "everyone deserves a second chance"; we loaned him back child support or added him to our cell phone plan that he promised to pay because we "trusted him" (clearly his children, their mother, the government, and former creditors learned the hard way what a mistake that was); and so forth.

As for those unfortunate qualities we can fix once he's ours? I'm sorry, but did he ever express an interest in being fixed? Or is he perfectly content with who he is, whether we think he should be or not? Not to mention, who exactly do we think we are to decide which qualities we'll allow him to keep and which ones we'll be overhauling, thank you? And let's face it, if some man started a relationship with us based not on how he feels about us but on who we'll be after he "fixes" us, we'd be livid. How dare we presume to (try to) do something to them that we ourselves wouldn't put up with for two seconds? On top of which, I repeat, and I promise this is the truth: *it doesn't work*. He'll change only if and when he wants to—just like us—and we have no right to expect anything else or anything less.

Instead, for a refreshing change of pace, how about if we start taking what I call The Inventory when we're first getting to know him, before we've fallen for him and we still have a few shreds of our wits about us? The Inventory is actually today's exercise: you're going to do an inventory on the heart-breaker, in your journal/diary/workbook. When you see the results on paper, ask yourself if you would really have proceeded into the relationship if you'd bothered to gather the information and then (that pesky part we so often prefer to skip over) *acted accordingly*. And you're never going to start another relationship without completing The Inventory first, by the way, so you might as well start practicing now.

The Inventory is a list of easy, basic questions about him, his habits, and his character that will speak volumes about the odds of your being happy with him for any length of time *just as he is, without your presumptuous, delusional fantasies of changing him*. And here's the part that's every bit as important, if not more so: if the odds of your being happy with "the real him" aren't good, move on! None of us, even as a rebound, want to end up with someone with whom we're unhappy and, as a result, essentially say to the world, "Yes, I really am this desperate to have a boyfriend."

All you have to do to learn the answers to these questions is listen closely to him, pay attention, and just plain observe with your eyes wide open instead of closed at your selective convenience. Again, write these into your journal/diary/workbook, add any of your own that are important to you, and then answer them *honestly* about your heartbreaker. They're not judgments, they're just worthwhile facts about who he is and who he's entitled to be if he wants to—or, to put it another way, "What was he like when you met him?"

- Is he reliable?
- Is he respectful of your friends, family, children, pets, and everyone else you value, whether he's met them or not?
- Does he have a solid work ethic?
- Is he addicted to anything, whether it's drugs, alcohol, his Xbox, or televised sports?
- Are his priorities compatible with yours?
- Is he bossy?
- Does he take responsibility for where he is in life, or is he more comfortable being a victim?
- Is he inherently honest?
- How well does he deal with a crisis?
- How is he at reciprocity?
- Is he flexible?
- Is he an authority on pretty much everything?
- Is it extremely important to him to be right?
- Is he tolerant?
- Is he an inherently helpful person?
- Is he successful (which has a variety of interpretations, obviously)?

- Is he generous?
- Are his sexual habits compatible with yours?
- Can you confidently "take him anywhere"?
- Is he a good sport about situations or activities that weren't his idea?
- Does he make you feel better about yourself when you're with him?
- Is he content to share the attention in a room?
- Have his past relationships been generally successful, or disastrous?
- Does he treat his friends and family well?
- Is he a bully?
- Does he do what he says he's going to do?
- Does he value your opinions?
- Does disagreeing with him invariably lead to an argument?
- Is he emotionally as strong as you are?
- Does he keep his promises?
- Are his hobbies and interests of interest to you?
- Do his priorities make sense to you?
- Does he prefer to have conversations or deliver monologues?
- Does he think it's appropriate to call you names?
- Is he only comfortable when he's in control?
- Does he enjoy his own company?
- Does he have his own full, stimulating life?
- Is he good at "taking care of business" rather than asking you to take care of it?

- Is he chronically punctual?
- Does he have any longstanding traditions he enjoys that you might be called upon to respect—watching sports on TV every Sunday, going out one night a week with "his boys," a golf or tennis match every Saturday, a monthly poker game?
- Does he take your work as seriously as he expects you to take his?
- Does he have a good track record when it comes to monogamy (if he cheated on someone else with you, the answer to that is no, whether you like it or not)?
- Do you have the same view on basic tidiness?
- If he sees you unloading groceries from the car, will he come help you without being asked?
- Does the word "integrity" hold the same importance for both of you?
- Do spirituality and religion hold the same importance for both of you, even if you might express them differently?

Again, please add questions of your own based on your preferences and priorities. But don't ignore the ones that might be uncomfortable. This exercise is ultimately designed to help you learn more about you, how you probably overlooked any number of qualities that made happiness with the heartbreaker impossible in the long run, and how—emotionally convenient or not—you can save yourself an enormous amount of pain in the future if you simply and honestly apply

The Inventory to every contender who comes along in the future.

You have every right to be exactly who you are, and to learn and grow and change at your own pace, based on your own experiences and preferences.

Respect his right to do the same.

And if that doesn't work for you, it's really simple: for your sake and his, just move on.

Today's Affirmation

(which says it far more beautifully than I ever could)

God grant me the serenity to accept the things I cannot change; the courage to change the things I can; and the wisdom to know the difference.

DAY 21

Calling All Drama Queens

What we both seemed to forget through all the games we played was that in every game someone has to lose.

—LINDSAY HARRISON

As you know if you've watched *One Life to Live* with any regularity in the past ten years, my character, Lindsay Rappaport, is a drama queen. She believes that the end justifies the means, and she's a consummate game player when it comes to relationships. She's also, by the way, a woman with a good heart who just wants love and security and doesn't understand why those things seem to come so much more easily to everyone else than they do to her. We all know as we watch her that she's shooting herself in the foot at every turn in pursuit of her perfectly normal goals, but the fact that she doesn't know that is part of what makes her so endearing and such a pleasure to play as an actress.

In real life, though, despite being a card-carrying soap diva, I find manufactured drama and game playing to be exhausting, confusing, and a waste of everyone's time. I believe we all go through quite enough drama in our lives without deliberately stirring it up, and while game playing might be very effective temporarily, it's never worth the long-term consequence. (Take it from Lindsay Rappaport.)

It's been my experience, with the character I play and with actual drama queens and game players I've known and loved, that the need to act out usually comes from a lot of insecurity and fear and an urge to feel better as soon as possible, if only for a minute or two.

And what situation is more likely to bring out more insecurity and fear and an urge to feel better than having your heart broken? It might be so gratifying to give him one last parting shot to make it crystal clear that he caused you pain. After all he's put you through, you deserve just a little more attention from him, and, as an added bonus, maybe you can teach him a lesson he won't easily forget.

I promise you, if you let your inner drama queen give in to that urge and take action, the only lesson you're likely to teach him is that he's better off without you.

It's amazing how common it is for some women (and yes, some men too, but we're not concerning ourselves with them right now) to let their anger and hurt override their better judgment, if only for a few minutes, in the aftermath of a breakup. They slash his tires, they vandalize his car, they destroy his belongings (sometimes but not always limited to the gifts they gave him), they show up at his house in the middle of the night unannounced and uninvited—the list is far longer than I can relate or care to imagine. But there are several things that those "harmless games" have in common that I truly want you to bear in mind if you find that any or all of them sound tempting.

They're all illegal. Yes, every one of them, including destroying gifts you gave him. The moment they passed from you to him in the form of a gift, they became as surely his property as if he'd bought them himself. And yes, including showing up at his house, no matter how many millions of times you may have been there before. If you're not expected or invited and he doesn't ask you to stay, you're trespassing. Any act on that list could result in your forfeiting your freedom, as if you haven't already been through quite enough. Or you could just end up losing in a civil suit and—how's this for not what you had in mind at all?—having to pay him for whatever you damaged or destroyed, as if the relationship hasn't already cost you enough. Of course, there's also the irony that, whether he admits it or not, he'll be a little flattered that he still has some power over your actions, you apparently can't get over him, and you still find him worth your time and energy. Do you really want to pay him that unintended compliment?

In the far bigger picture, however, even on the off-chance that there are no legal repercussions, it breaks my heart to think of you letting anyone, ever, and most of all someone who broke your heart, compromise your dignity and integrity for a single moment. No one is worth that. Again, *no one is worth that.*

I heard a wonderful observation years ago that I think of often. It's on the subject of crisis, and let's face it, having your heart broken is a crisis. The saying goes, "Crisis doesn't build character, it reveals it." One of my many wishes for you is that you see to it that this crisis will reveal nothing more and nothing less than the finest, strongest, most self-controlled, liberated, and graceful character you possess.

Today's Exercise

If you really can't resist fantasizing about the creative array of games and dramas you'd like to play out in your heartbreaker's face, by all means, take out your journal/diary/workbook and write them down. Go into every diabolical detail, and have a great time.

Just one condition, though: at the end of each one of them, you have to think of and describe in an equal amount of detail the worst possible short-term and long-term consequences you could be setting yourself up for if you were to act out the fantasy.

If you're really honest and really thorough about the second part of this exercise, I promise you won't need me to tell you again that he's just not worth it, and you're worth far, far more.

Today's Affirmation

Today I have taken another step toward loving myself completely, regarding myself with pride and honor, my intellect perfectly cemented with my emotions so that I will never and would never again deface and defame my own integrity in any way.

DAY 22

Learning to Look Ahead

The greatest predictor of the future is the past.
—Dr. Phil McGraw

We women tend to like instant gratification.

We like romance.

And we don't like practicality and cold, hard facts to interfere with either of the above, thank you.

Which I truly believe significantly contributes to many of our poor choices and our often resolute refusal to look ahead and anticipate a future that any objective observer would see coming a mile away. (Not that we would listen to warnings anyway, of course. That's another thing about us: we're not just stupid and blind when we're in love, we're deaf as well, and no matter how time-worn the cliché we fall into, or how overwhelming the statistics against certain relationships we say yes to, we insist on believing that somehow or other, we are the exception.)

Wouldn't it be wonderful, and save us untold future heartache, if we could train ourselves to put our passions for instant gratification and romance aside in the first days of our next relationship and look ahead, with all the practicality and objectivity we can muster? If we could (and I know we can if we set our minds to it), it's very likely that a lot of our potential "I'd love to's" would turn into much smarter and healthier "No, thank you's."

To illustrate through the use of an extreme but not uncommon example: let's say you meet an incredibly attractive man who's equally attracted to you. You like everything about him except for one thing: he's married. But to your surprise, you're tempted to pursue a relationship with him anyway, to see where this might lead.

Don't worry, I'm not going to launch into a morality lecture here. That's between you and your conscience. I'm not going to point out that by simply being married and asking you out, he's already revealed himself as a liar and a cheater with no regard whatsoever for the woman he married, who probably also happens to be the mother of his children. There's a real dream-come-true kind of a guy. . . . Nor am I going to even mention the predictability of his description of his marriage: she doesn't understand him; she's a relentless, impossible, nagging shrew; their sex life is virtually nonexistent; there's been no love between them for years. Mind you, there's very possibly not much truth to any of that, but what else is he supposed to say when he's trying to convince himself, and you, that he has perfectly good reasons for being unfaithful? On the other hand, if you were home alone with the children while he was out cheating on you, you might not exactly greet him with open arms when he comes crawling home either.

Which leads very neatly to my proposed exercise of making yourself stop and look ahead before you start. Look way ahead—to this scenario, for example.

You've been going out with him for, let's say, almost a year, and it's heaven—the stolen moments, the clandestine getaways, the sheer heightened emotion of romance unencumbered by the fact that someone else, not you, gets to be in charge of his dirty socks and his bad moods and his kids' flu and his bill paying. And then one day, your fondest wish comes true and he shows up on your doorstep with his luggage. It's true, he's left her, and he's left her for you. That's undoubtedly not the reason he gave her, but what difference does it make? You're going to be together now, sleeping together in the same bed all night long, night after night, as the two of you fantasized about so often. You won, he's yours now, and you'll never be unhappy again.

A month goes by, and it's all going beautifully. And then, early one evening, you're hard at work making his favorite meal to surprise him, when the phone rings. It's him. He couldn't be sorrier to be calling like this on such short notice, but a potential client he's been pursuing forever has just arrived in town for the night and asked him to meet him at his hotel for dinner. If it were anyone else he would have said no, but you know how important this client could be. He hears the disappointment in your voice, and he's so sorry, but he promises he'll make it up to you. He's so sweet and apologetic and excited that you assure him it's really okay, and you wish him luck with his meeting.

You're eating his favorite meal all by yourself in front of the TV when it slowly starts to hit you. That call he just made to you sounded exactly like the occasional calls he made to his wife from your apartment so the two of you could have a few more hours together before he had to head home. There was no last-minute dinner with a potential client then. What if there isn't one now either? Why on earth would you believe him? You happen to have firsthand expertise at what an inventive storyteller he is and, for that matter, how meaningless monogamy is to him. The truth is, based on your own experience, you don't have the first clue where he really is, or whom he's really with. And as long as you're with him, you never will. Every time he walks out that door, you'll wonder, no matter how sincere he is when he reassures you that he loves you and he would never cheat on you—exactly what he undoubtedly told her—his wife, the mother of his children. . . .

In the end, what a sad life to set up for yourself, and that's the supposed dream-come-true version. It's much more likely that he'll make a thousand excuses for never leaving her at all, which in its own way will be equally painful for you.

Or, if you force yourself to logically, practically, unromantically look ahead at the facts, not the fantasy, before it's too late, you'll spare yourself every minute of that doomed future and *just say no* the first time and every time he asks.

*   *   *

As I said, it's an extreme high-drama example. But I hope it illustrates the point of working on a whole new skill, the skill of projecting far enough down the line to take a realistic look at your life inside any future relationships that come along. Of course, feel free to do the same with your relationship with your heartbreaker, even though you obviously know how that came out, if only to see whether you might have stopped yourself before you started if you'd had this skill to work with.

Today's Exercise

I want you to start practicing this skill right now, so that by the time you meet someone new and think you might be interested, you've already made it a habit to realistically look ahead and see how life with this man might look a year from now, based purely on facts.

All you have to do is take out your journal/diary/workbook and, off the top of your head, write down five occupations and circumstances of potential men in your future—"widowed fireman with two young children," for example, or "newly divorced bartender with no children."

Then, project yourself into the most probable theoretical dream-come-true reality of your life with him, let's say, a year from now. Go into as much detail as the married man story, starting with something like, "My parents, who are very important to me, have just arrived in town to meet him for the first time. He, his children, my parents, and I are being seated at my favorite restaurant when he gets an emergency call to go to work." If you're someone who needs a structured, orderly, predictable life—and, as an added bonus, you've never especially wanted children—this is not likely to be a successful relationship for any of you. If, on the other hand, you're comfortable with spontaneity, you're proud of him, you understand the demands of his job, and you love children, it could be very much worth pursuing.

As I said, do five of these now to get a feel for the skill, and keep doing more as you think of them in the days and weeks ahead. Ideally, you'll get into the habit and never start another relationship without looking ahead first and giving yourself the best possible odds that it will succeed.

Today's Affirmation

I will find ways to remind myself each and every day that the choices I make today, no matter how much or how little thought I put into them, create the realities I'll be living in tomorrow.

DAY 23

Running into Him

Nobody can make you feel inferior without your consent.

—Eleanor Roosevelt

It's almost inevitable: sooner or later, unless one or the other of you moves far, far away, you're going to run into your heartbreaker again.

I know you've abided by the no contact rules we talked about, and I hope you've avoided his favorite places to spare yourself one of those peril-fraught "accidental" encounters.

I also know you've imagined about a thousand different scenarios of what will happen and how you'll handle that first meeting. In some scenarios you're cool and aloof while he tells you that losing you was the biggest mistake of his life. In others *he's* cool and aloof and you give him that piece of your mind you've been rehearsing to perfection. In still others you're making a quick dash to the corner drugstore for shampoo, looking every bit as unshowered as you are, and want to die as he walks right by with his new girlfriend, who bears an uncanny resemblance to Angelina Jolie. And on your better days there's the one where he's sitting alone and forlorn in a restaurant with an unavoidable view of you, done to perfection, being showered with adoration by your date, a dead ringer for David Beckham.

It's the most normal thing in the world to try to anticipate the best and the worst about upcoming events that matter to us, to give us the feeling of being prepared for anything. But I swear there's nothing to be gained from trying to convince ourselves how we're going to feel at that moment when we first see him again and have to juggle all that familiarity, all those memories, all that grief we've been battling and our new, painful, seemingly miscast role as an ex. When the moment actually happens, there's no amount of preparation in the world that will dictate how you react.

To prove that point and several others, to inspire you, and to make you smile, I'm going to share the absolutely true story of a friend of mine, for which she's given me her enthusiastic permission, with the added message, "If it can happen to me, it can happen to anyone."

My friend, a scriptwriter, had been with her boyfriend for six years when they broke up. She'd invested a whole lot of her heart and soul and time and energy in him, though they maintained separate residences, and she was devastated when he left, with the same all-consuming dark grief we've all been through. I didn't know her then, but she didn't need me to give her the no contact rule. She's never been one to pursue a man, especially when he's walked out the door, so there were no phone calls, no drives past his house, no "just wanted to say hi" chats with his friends, no mention of him during conversations with their mutual friends. No nothing, just deafening silence and her unsuccessful efforts to work, or sleep, or care.

After two months of virtual paralysis, and getting very concerned about her inability to concentrate enough to write scripts, i.e., pay her mortgage, she got a referral from a friend for a good clinical psychologist in the hope of some serious, much needed help just to feel like some version of herself again.

She arrived compulsively (and desperately) early for her first therapy session and, too nervous to amuse herself in a waiting room full of back issues of *Psychology Today*, she headed to the coffee shop in the lobby of her therapist's office building. She was sitting at the counter, mindlessly buttering a piece of toast she had no intention of eating, when, from a few stools away, she heard a male voice tentatively call her name.

She looked over and instantly recognized a successful television producer whose work she'd always admired. She managed a smile and said hello, shocked that he recognized her (to this day she cherishes the anonymity of being a writer) and even more shocked when he told her he was a fan of her work as well. They talked for several minutes until she had to leave for her appointment, and she and the producer exchanged business cards as they said good-bye. Bearing in mind how depressed she was and how many other more pressing issues were occupying her mind, it's no surprise that she barely gave the producer another thought as she settled into her first therapy session.

The therapist was a godsend, a brilliant, practical, insightful woman, and my friend began seeing her, and feeling increasingly more functional, every week, rain or shine, come hell or high water.

In the meantime, about a month after that first passing chat in the coffee shop, the producer called with a project he wanted her to write. She gratefully accepted, with a lot of silent prayers that her talent might be willing to come out of hiding again by now—she wanted to work with this gifted man and, even more relevant, she needed the money.

The project was thoroughly enjoyable and very demanding, and it went so well that an offer for another one with the same producer immediately followed. With her bank account restored to health, and in good mental health as well, thanks to her ongoing therapy, she was even able to remodel the kitchen of her beloved little house, something she'd been yearning to do for years.

One day she was cooking lunch for herself on her gorgeous new Viking oven in her gorgeous new kitchen when the doorbell rang. She was sure it was the messenger she was expecting, so she opened the door without asking who it was.

And there, after a year and a half, stood the man who'd broken her heart.

Like the rest of us, she'd imagined this moment a million times, with a million variations, most of which involved her embarrassing herself by bursting into tears. But she'd never imagined him at her door, and she'd certainly never imagined this: out of nothing but total shock, she laughed, then stepped back and invited him in.

"So," he said with mock nonchalance, "what have you been up to?"

She looked him right in the eye with a smile and replied, "You go first."

He'd been up to a few things, actually, which didn't surprise her—he'd always been a busy, successful man with a full, interesting life. It didn't escape her notice that he was gazing around at her new kitchen, visibly impressed, and that he did a double-take when he happened to spot and read the title page of her script, with her name prominently displayed beside the producer's, whom her heartbreaker had certainly heard of.

He wasn't there to reconcile, he'd just been thinking about her and wanted to say hello before he left for a six-month trip to England. (And how like him, she thought, to feel entitled to show up at her door unannounced after a year and a half.) He only stayed for fifteen minutes, and then, same as always, he whirled off to a meeting for which he was already late.

She closed the door and silently leaned against it, a thousand thoughts running through her mind—each one of which you're to remember and put to good use as your exercise for today:

"No wonder I was so shocked to see him. I've been so busy I don't even remember the last time I thought about him for more than a second or two."

"Thank you, God, from the bottom of my heart that the woman he dropped in on is healthy, happy, and busy, making a lot of progress in her life he couldn't help but notice, instead of that hollow, heartbroken, immobile shell of a woman who was living here a year and a half ago."

"Come to think of it, in a way I should have thanked *him*, for leaving me—his leaving me was what led me to my therapist, which is what led to the producer in the coffee shop. In fact, that breakup is one of the *best* things that ever happened to me! Who knew?!"

Last but certainly not least, and I truly want you to take this in rather than just read it for the billionth time in your life:

"What do you know, it's true after all. Success really is the best revenge!"

Today's Affirmation

Today I know more surely than ever that being productively busy is its own reward, that moving forward will always get me somewhere even when I don't feel like it, and that no matter how predictable I think life has become, there are great surprises being created for me right this minute and all I have to do to make them happen is be patient and stay out of my own way.

DAY 24

Personality Types Part 1: Mr. Wonderful

If it sounds too good to be true, it is.

—Anonymous

Like most of you, I'm willing to bet, I've chosen far more of my relationships by giving my heart free rein and telling my head to take a hike. I wasn't about to let my brain step in and ruin all the fun, nosiree. While letting our hearts overrule our heads sounds like such a gorgeous, gauze-covered, slow-motion, romantic pinnacle to give in to, you and I have found out the hard way that in real day-to-day life, we can and need to do better for ourselves from now on.

In our defense, I don't believe any of us were encouraged nearly enough to make educated choices in our personal lives. (I'm not even sure we were encouraged to recognize that our personal lives *involved* making choices.) I believe formal education is designed to prepare us to earn a living as best it can, and then, since by definition we won't be in school all by ourselves, we'll be exposed to a variety of other people every day and figure out the social aspects of life somehow—through trial and error, maybe. Or not. I really do think that's a shame.

Looking back, I can't help but smile with fond compassion at that woman I once was, who thought my relationship job was to be the best, most cheerful, most cooperative girlfriend/wife I could be and just take the ride I'd signed on to with men whose behavior seemed so haphazard and confusing, that sometimes I honestly felt I was losing my mind. I knew virtually nothing about myself—my *head* self, my long-term needs, my priorities, my goals, my boundaries—and understood even less that there really are general, legitimate personality types out there that we can watch out for and that make someone else's behavior not seem nearly so haphazard, not to mention *my fault*, after all.

What a relief to find that out! I swear I used to stand there gaping at some form of seemingly unmotivated insanity or other in a boyfriend or husband and think to myself, *Do I bring this out in people?!* But what do you know, it had little if anything to do with me and far more to do with his psychological makeup and any number of other factors in his psyche that only he could control, change, or affect. The more I learned, and continue to learn, about the psychological facts of various personality types, the more comforted I feel about what I used to perceive as past failures. There are some types I'm just plain more vulnerable to than others and should avoid.

I'm more courageous about every new potential friend, date, or relationship that comes along. It doesn't feel like a roll of the dice anymore. And also, finally, it encourages my head to participate again in the choices I make, rather than relying on nothing but my soft, naïve, easily misguided heart.

In this chapter and the next two, then, I'm going to share overviews of three very common personality types out there. I guarantee some of them will sound familiar to you, from your past and probably from among the people around you every day right now. Please don't read them as indictments; after all, we women have our personality types too. Simply read them as another starter course in your ongoing education about insuring yourself a future of healthy, empowering love, joy, happiness, and peace of mind. And again I say, never let your earnest, impulsive heart convince you to settle for anything less than that.

Mr. Wonderful

Mr. Wonderful is such a clichéd notion, and such clichéd behavior, that it's amazing that any of us still fall for it. But we do. We'll keep right on doing it until we wise up and knock it off. In the meantime, count on it, men will keep right on with this silly facade as long as we keep proving to them time and time again that it works.

Mr. Wonderful comes swaggering in out of nowhere and, in record time, appeals to our romanticized emotions and egos by telling us how beautiful we are, and how funny, and how smart, and how talented. They've never heard anything as interesting in their lives as what we have to say, they haven't met anyone as special as we are in so long that they'd given up on trying to find someone like us—until now. They can't believe their luck, especially after all they've been through (poor babies), that we've come along. As added bonuses, they're usually bright, articulate, and relatively attractive, and, like all self-respecting White Knights, they seem like good guys we could proudly take to dinner with any group of friends or to our next family reunion.

It will usually be on about the third or fourth date, long before you've gone through even a fraction of your wardrobe, that Mr. Wonderful will say something like this: "You know, if I'm not careful, I could fall in love with you." He'll back up that statement too, with a lot of phone calls, e-mails, and togetherness, and before you even have time to get your bearings, you've been swept right off your feet (which, now that I really picture that, pretty much puts us on our butts, doesn't it?).

It's all so darling, so flattering, and so overwhelming that, unless we're secure with our own identities and well informed about his, we won't even recognize a fact that's bound to disappoint us as the relationship wears on: Mr. Wonderful is in reality a *dependent personality*. The compliments, the attention, the oh-so-soon use of the word "love" are intended to dazzle us so much that we won't even notice what's really dazzling us is a big, twinkling row of red flags. We're being lured and engaged, and the currency that's attracting us is our own willingness to believe they mean all that flattery. It's like we're being bought with our own chips, and we're too enchanted to notice.

The big thud lurking in the future with Mr. Wonderful is the fact that what started out seeming to be about us and our infinitely interesting thoughts and lives invariably turns out to be entirely, completely, and exhaustively about them. Securing our rapt, adoring attention was simply their way of insuring that they've found an answer to their neediness. Once we've agreed to be that answer, usually at the expense of our own priorities, we discover that all those compliments turn into criticism when we're not being our old attentive selves; our thoughts and lives aren't remotely interesting if they interfere with his needs, opinions, and preferences; and frankly, while he would never admit it (or perhaps even know it), what he was really looking for wasn't a girlfriend at all—it was some combination of a mom, an audience, and an obligated play-mate.

And really, don't you have something better to do with your valuable time?

The most efficient way to spot Mr. Wonderful ASAP, before your heart has shoved your head out of the way, is to keep reminding yourself of one unavoidable, undeniable fact: in a few short weeks or months, he just plain doesn't know you well enough to be coming to any grand conclusions about who you are, what you're like, and, above all, how much in love with you he's already fallen. You're far more fabulous than all his compliments suggest, and far more complex than he's begun to imagine, but since he has no way of knowing that yet, take it from an actress: *it's just dialogue.* Remember, anybody can say anything, especially when it serves their purpose. And a real, decent, truly good man would never compromise his credibility or disrespect your intelligence, luring you into a relationship with uninformed flattery and behavior so attentive that he hopes you won't think to ask yourself, *Why does he have this much free time on his hands?* The answer: because he's Mr. Wonderful, in search of someone to provide him with the life he's too needy and dependent to provide for himself.

That someone isn't you. After all you've been through and all you're in the process of learning, you honor yourself far too much for that nonsense. And you have no idea how proud I am of you for that.

I believe that's quite enough for today. Draw your well-deserved *X* through Day 24 on your calendar, and I'll meet you back here tomorrow. You can count on it!

Today's Affirmation

Today I commit to treating my increasing wisdom as the gift that it is by honoring my life with only those who sincerely honor it right along with me. My soul is learning more every day, and joyfully celebrating the vast but subtle difference between noise and substance, and it's a lesson of power I won't forget again.

DAY 25

Personality Types Part 2: Controller-Manipulators

*An effective way to deal with predators is to
taste terrible.*

—Anonymous

I have a great longtime pal named Willie—truly just a pal, never a romantic thought between us; his wife, Judy, is a good friend as well.

One day I arrived in a restaurant parking lot to meet him for lunch and found him standing by his car, looking chagrined, not talking on his cell phone so much as holding it a few inches from his ear as his wife yelled at him on the other end of the line. While she yelled, he quietly explained to me that he'd locked his keys in his car and had called Judy to ask her to drive over with the spare set. To put it mildly, she didn't want to.

When they'd finally finished what we'll politely call their

discussion, Willie hung up and said, a little wistfully, "When Judy and I were dating, she thought I was adorable and eccentric when I'd do something like this. After twenty-eight years of marriage it's one of the things she hates most about me."

I've thought about that comment a hundred times since that day and realized that we women really do like to put the most endearing spin on potential red flags when we have our hearts set on giving our hearts away. With one of the good guys, like Willie, it amounts to nothing but an "oh, well." But with a controller-manipulator, we can be spinning and euphemizing ourselves into a desperately unhappy, crazy-making, suffocating—even dangerous—trap.

Controller-Manipulators

You've either heard the euphemisms or used them yourself a hundred times when a really skilled controller-manipulator comes along:

"It's so sweet, he just wants to know where I am and what I'm doing every single minute!"

"The connection between us is so intense that he can't stand for us to be apart."

"He loves me so much that he doesn't want to share me with anyone else."

"If I don't return his calls/texts/e-mails within five minutes, he freaks out. I've never met anyone so protective/caring/attentive/vigilant/flattering."

And of course no one but the woman in love is surprised

when, after a few months or years, all that spin winds down and the euphemisms are replaced with cold, hard facts.

"He has to control every move I make."

"He's smothering me."

"He won't even let me see my family and friends."

"I don't feel loved; I feel trapped."

It's such a breeze to see when we're on the outside looking in, but when it comes to controller-manipulators we usually can't even accuse them of the old bait and switch, where their behavior does a complete flip from Dr. Jekyll to Mr. Hyde. The really adept controller-manipulator tends to give plenty of previews for everything we have to look forward to if we buy into them. They just leave out the warnings that it's only going to expand and intensify, and that once the early rush of newness, sweet talk, pillow talk, and plain old showing off is over with, you've given permission for as much controlling and manipulating as they care to dish out and, therefore, you have no right to complain.

Not that complaining would be worth your effort anyway. Controller-manipulators are not notoriously empathetic listeners. Instead, their responses to complaints, no matter how justified, are likely to range from pouting to yelling to full-blown tantrums to retaliatory bursts of name-calling and suggestions that what you're complaining about is actually your fault to begin with—if you'd only pay attention/do what you're told/cooperate/try harder/think about *them* for a change, the two of you wouldn't be having these problems to begin with. Especially after (all together now) *all they do for you*!

I recently interviewed a bright, beautiful, successful career woman who, several years earlier, had met a very charming, very handsome, equally successful airline pilot. In the course of their whirlwind romance she was nothing but flattered when he showered her with expensive gifts and fantasy dates; seemed to feel competitive with anything that took her attention away from him, from her dog to her favorite TV shows to attentive waiters to her job to her friends and family, because he "loved her so much"; moved her from her quaint, charming, convenient apartment into his impressive country house that was miles and miles from everyone she knew; proposed within a few months; and insisted she quit her job so that she could get some long-overdue relaxation and he could take care of her. And, he assured her with his most endearing laugh, he would personally see to it that being his wife would be a full-time job all by itself.

It was all thrilling and overwhelming and fabulously busy—so busy, in fact, that she didn't have time, or *take* time, to think. She just "followed her heart" (i.e., sent her brain on vacation) and before long found herself isolated with him in his beautiful but remote house separated from a job she'd enjoyed that had given her a sense of purpose and accomplishment, feeling perpetually obligated to him because, at his insistence, she was making no financial contribution to the household (invariably letting his preferences override hers to avoid his inevitable whining and arguing), driving the car he bought her (but titled solely in his name), and wearing the clothes she bought with the allowance he gave her (but only if they were clothes he approved of).

Most devastating of all to her was finding herself estranged from the family and friends she'd always adored and relied on for emotional nourishment. It wasn't that they'd abandoned her. She'd essentially abandoned them, not because she didn't miss them terribly but because (a) he didn't care for them and couldn't be relied on not to make that clear when he was around them; (b) when she was alone with them he resented the time she was spending away from him, which she knew he'd be pouting about when she got home; and (c) she found her end of the conversations to be stilted and heavily edited out of embarrassment over a stifling marriage to a man they'd all found loving ways to warn her about when the whirlwind courtship began.

In case you're wondering about his friends, by the way, there were very few of them—because of his work schedule, or because *she* alienated them, or because of anything but him. Are you getting the picture?

Probably the most definitive tradition of their marriage, though, occurred when he (an airline pilot, don't forget) would fly over their house on his way home from a trip and flash the lights on the 747 to cue her that it was time for her to leave for the airport to come pick him up—and keeping him waiting was not an acceptable option.

Like all dutiful controller-manipulators, he became a virtual master of hypocrisy, criticizing and demeaning her for exactly the circumstances she'd agreed to in order to please him. She was "lazy" and "unmotivated" and "sponging" off him— her thanks for cooperating with his insistence that she quit her job, devote her life to being married to him, and let him take care of her. As her self-confidence and sense of meaningful purpose in life eroded, replaced by stress and depression, she lost a frightening amount of weight and started looking pinched, drawn, and ten years older than she was—which he was only too happy to point out and complain about, which only made it worse. He also informed her on more than one occasion how lucky she was to have him, because as lazy and haggard-looking as she was, no one else would want her. And since she'd pushed her beloved support system of friends and family away out of embarrassment, they weren't there to tell her how wrong he was, so she began to believe him.

Every once in a great while her frustration would spill over and she would tell him she was thinking of leaving him. Sometimes it would provoke him to double up on the insults at the top of his lungs. But on other occasions he would pull out another favorite weapon of the controller-manipulator: sympathy. He would begin to cry, reminding her of the pain he still suffered over his mother abandoning the family when he was only nine years old. If that childhood tragedy caused him to be too overbearing or possessive toward his wife, it was only because he loved her so much and his fear of losing her overrode his better judgment. He was sorry, but he couldn't help it.

And she, not wanting to cause him pain on top of all the other misery she was already feeling, would mentally unpack her bags and ride it out for a while longer.

It took her eight years to finally become determined enough, angry enough, and sick and tired enough of being sick and tired, to get herself out of there. She started by opening up to her friends and family, dropping the "everything's fine" facade, and telling them the truth. Sure enough, they'd been there all along, loving her and waiting for her if she'd only let them back in again. She still remembered when I talked to her several years after her divorce how starved she'd been for the emotional nourishment, support, and—oh, my God—*laughter* that had been at her beck and call every minute of those eight long years. She also remembered one of her friends saying, after hearing a description of the constant criticism and control she'd been subjected to, "As my therapist suggested when I was trying to decide whether to leave *my* marriage, 'When you find yourself in a no-win situation over and over again, *stop playing*!' " It was the lightbulb-over-the-head that finally pushed her out the door, and despite all his accusations and tantrums and tears and threats and predictions of failure without him, she never looked back.

She's now a happy and successful registered nurse, looks five years younger than her age, wishes she could lose a few pounds but isn't worried about it, and has been dating a great guy for four years who's in no more of a hurry to move in together or get married than she is.

She looks back and shakes her head at all the red flags she missed or euphemized for the sake of romance. And I gave her my word that I would share her story so that all of us who might refuse to pay attention to those same red flags when a skilled controller-manipulator comes along can learn from her well-intentioned but misplaced eagerness to be loved.

Today's Affirmation
(just like yesterday's, to make sure it sinks in)

Today I commit to treating my increasing wisdom as the gift that it is by honoring my life with only those who sincerely honor it right along with me.

DAY 26

Personality Types Part 3: A Cavalcade of Losers

If you don't stand for something, you'll fall for anything.

—Anonymous

One night while watching a TV news magazine show I found myself gaping at an interview with the author of a how-to book on easy, breezy techniques for men to subtly coerce women into doing their emotional and sexual bidding. Apparently the man who graced society with this literary gem makes a substantial living conducting very expensive seminars to other men who can't attract a woman through any other means but deception, cruel games, and a complete absence of integrity. It hurt my soul to watch it. I remember thinking, *Gee, his mom must be so proud.*

Curious to know what the little boys in grown-up costumes were up to, I bought the book. And frankly, the only thing more shocking than the tactics this book recommends is the fact that some women are actually falling for them.

The basic reverse-psychology gist these losers use goes like this:

They stake out places, especially bars, where women are likely to gather in groups. After studying the basic body language within the group to determine relative vulnerability, lack of self-confidence, etc., they approach and engage them in casual conversation. During this conversation one of the losers puts on an imaginary classic bad-boy hat, turns to one of the more vulnerable women, and tosses out an insult, something along the lines of, "You know, just because they sell that outfit in your size doesn't mean you should wear it," or, "So tell me, is acting like an airhead really working for you?"

This is guaranteed to provoke one of two responses. The self-confident woman who commands and demands common courtesy and respect will respond with some version of, "Drop dead!" and walk away. Sadly, the vulnerable, uncertain woman who's so eager to be liked that she'll reduce herself to striving for acceptance even from this waste of protoplasm will actually rise to the challenge of winning him over. Next thing you know she's actually responding to him as if he's worth dignifying with a response, and he's reeling her in like a marlin. He set her up to be needy, she bought it, and off they go into what she'll probably try to pretend is a relationship and what at best he'll think of as a protracted booty call.

What we know that this poor woman is forgetting is that (a) we never win someone's respect by tolerating disrespect;

(b) over time behavior in a relationship tends to get worse, not better, so it's guaranteed that what she has to look forward to is downhill from a cheap shot; and (c) Dr. Phil says it best—we really do teach people how to treat us.

I'm not about to recommend this book and put even more money into this author's pocket. (In fact, I was so creeped out by the contribution I grudgingly made when I bought my copy that I matched the price of the book with a donation to one of my favorite animal charities.) But I insist on using it as a handy guide for us women who take ourselves and our lives seriously by offering what the police call a BOLO, short for Be On the Look-Out. So, be on the look-out for:

- A slight facade of arrogance and swagger, meant to imply superiority.
- The (accurate) feeling in his presence that you're being sized up like a used car rather than appreciated as a potential girlfriend.
- Odd feelings of defensiveness, confusion, and imbalance in his presence.
- His saying, "I was kidding," or accusing you of having no sense of humor, when/if you take exception to a careless or insulting comment.
- An almost involuntary need to beg for those compliments he so deliberately withholds.
- Mixed signals from him, edgy conversation, and insults during body language designed to indicate that he's interested.

- Feeling worse about yourself rather than better, and more insecure than secure, after spending time with him.

As a friend of mine says, with sarcasm, any one of those signs is "such a lovely quality in a date." And remember, none of them can work for the losers at those seminars if we don't let them. So I want to hear an "Amen!" followed by a resounding, "Drop dead!"

It doesn't stop there, of course. There are several other personality types out there I want to briefly summarize before we move on, to make sure you're forewarned, forearmed, and confident that it never was and it never will be *just you!*

The Narcissist

You can almost sit back and put your feet up when dealing with the narcissist, because everything is always about nothing but *him*—every conversation, every choice of restaurant and movie, every event no matter how trivial is of no value unless it somehow relates to him. He sees people as nothing but walking mirrors in which to admire himself. As long as he's flattered by the reflection of himself in your eyes, you'll be of value to him. But the minute you catch on that what you're looking at is all form and no substance, he'll react in one of two ways: he'll either disappear as quickly as possible or he'll repeat whatever performance won your approval in the first place, purely for the exercise of winning again.

Here's a true story that could be called "Portrait of a Narcissist."

I briefly worked with an actor who was almost artistic in his ability to turn every conversation, no matter what the topic, into a conversation about him. It became a source of fascination for me and the rest of the cast, because he was really brilliant at it, but once the novelty wore off it became downright tedious.

One morning a group of us were sitting around waiting to start filming, and somehow or other we wandered onto the subject of the Holocaust. It was during this obviously serious, grim discussion that I noticed the actor in question approaching us, and I had the fleeting thought that finally we'd come up with a conversation he couldn't possibly insinuate himself into.

I was wrong. He stood beside me for a few moments getting the gist of the subject matter and then proudly announced, "You know, I'm very big in Germany."

There you have it. The essence of the narcissist, a quick, informative glimpse into how their mind works, no matter who you are, what you do, or how hard you try. He'll reveal himself early on if you simply listen closely for the inappropriate frequency of the words "I" and "me."

The bottom line you have to look forward to with the narcissist can be found in the phrase I used in that story: once the novelty wears off he'll become downright tedious.

The Bully

Just like on playgrounds around the world, the bully will do his best to intimidate and boss around anyone who'll tolerate it. At first he may treat you beautifully, because he's interested and on his best behavior. But pay close attention to his treatment of waiters, salespeople, coworkers (especially if he has employees), valets, and other people you're likely to come across early in your relationship. If he's pleasant, respectful, and gracious to them, good for him. If he's abrupt, superior, rude, short-tempered, and cruel, he's got a mean streak in him, and you're looking at the treatment you and your family and friends have to look forward to once he feels secure enough to put his best-behavior phase behind him.

Don't waste any more time trying to analyze why and how he became a bully than you spent wondering about that very thing on the playground. Just assure yourself that you haven't put all this effort into your full, rich, potential-filled life to waste a single moment of it being someone's verbal punching bag.

The Histrionic

This is the man who has unapologetically poor impulse control. He bangs on his steering wheel and screams in agonized rage at the slightest traffic infraction; he throws a tantrum the size of Asia over anything from a bad haircut to his house burning down as if they're of equal gravity; he "creates scenes" at the drop of a hat out of sheer boredom and habit: The words "no big deal" are completely foreign to him, and because his own emotional release is more important to him than maintaining the integrity of the environment he's in, he'll have no concern about who's around, who he might embarrass, who he might frighten, or who he might offend when he "goes off."

Unless you're every bit as histrionic as he is and this kind of perpetual lit-fuse existence appeals to you, you know from past experience that anyone who can't take minor frustrations in stride can't maintain a healthy relationship. So save yourself a lot of hysteria and heartache and tell him to get back to you when and if he can show you his anger management diploma.

The Perpetual Victim

This is another one who's easy to spot fairly quickly if you know what to listen for: he's been subjected to a whole lot of tragedy and injustice in his life, and amazingly, not one bit of it was his fault. From his abusive or absent parents to his cheating whore of an ex-girlfriend to his ex-wife who never appreciated him to his ex-boss who fired him for no good reason to anyone and everyone else in the long-suffering story of his life, this man isn't responsible for a single thing that's ever happened to him, although God knows he's done nothing but try his darnedest and generally been an all-around great guy.

Here's a quick, easy test to give him if you start suspecting you've got a diehard victim on your hands: during one of his inevitable tragic-past-relationship stories in which he's describing how horrible she was to him despite his flawlessly perfect treatment of her, casually observe, "Although I always find that if you look closely, it takes two people, not just one, to make or break a relationship, don't you think?" If he takes offense, even subtly, at the mere suggestion that something might have been even slightly his fault, and that you're not really buying into the depth of sympathy he was hoping for, congratulations. Chances are you've just made it onto his perpetrators list, where you're guaranteed to stay for as long as you continue to put up with a grown man who has no clue about or interest in the word "responsibility."

And hey, won't *that* be fun?

The World's Foremost Authority

There is nothing in this man's world that he doesn't happen to have an opinion about and—what are the odds?—every one of those opinions just happens to be *right*! Have you ever heard Dr. Phil ask one of his more pompous guests, "Would you rather be right or happy?" This man would rather be right, no matter how wrong all the evidence might prove him to be.

The trick is, he can deliver his rightness with such certainty, arrogance, and longevity that you might actually confuse him with an intellectual, or at the very least someone who knows what he's talking about. He doesn't carry on conversations; he delivers a series of absolutes, with an underlying tone that anyone who disagrees with him is an idiot. Whether it's a presidential candidate, a baseball team, a restaurant, a movie, a TV show, a singer, an actor, an author, an article of clothing, a car, a wine label, a grocery store, an artist, a European country, or a brand of paper towels, his favorite happens to be the only one that a person with a brain should even be bothered with, and he'll be happy to tell you why, at exhaustive length, until, if you're paying attention to your instincts, you get so tired of the mere sound of his voice you could scream.

And just think, starting a relationship will put you next in line for critiques from this windbag! Oh, boy!

Because no matter how intelligent and well-informed *your* opinions and preferences might be, there's no way around this one simple fact: the world's foremost authority's ego relies on being *right*, nothing more, nothing less, so there's no future in disagreeing with him. He'll do whatever he has to do to defend his position, having nothing to do with the usually trivial issue at hand and everything to do with maintaining his inexplicably high opinion of himself.

If a lifetime of "yes, dear" is right up your alley, this is the man for you. If not, excuse yourself to the ladies' room and then race to the nearest exit.

So many personality types, so little time. In three days I've only given you the highlights of a few of the men you're probably either recovering from or about to meet. I hope you'll keep exploring this subject through the vast array of fascinating books that are available, a few of which I'll mention in tomorrow's chapter, written by experts and authors with far more expertise than me.

In the meantime, no matter what personality types are waiting in your future for you to choose from, don't you ever forget:

Only with respect, honor, integrity, honesty, and love that enhances rather than limits your life can any man earn his way to your heart from now on.

One More Time

Today I commit to treating my increasing wisdom as the gift that it is by honoring my life with only those who sincerely honor it right along with me.

DAY 27

You Are So Beautiful

I wish you the most exquisite beauty of all:
soaring with confidence, untarnished by vanity,
in search of no one's approval but your own.

—Lindsay Harrison

You know one of my favorite things about being a woman? I wake up first thing in the morning, go scuffing into the bathroom, and inevitably find myself staring at myself in the mirror. If I were a man, I'd be staring at pretty much as good as it's going to get all day. But because I'm a woman, I can transform myself by creating almost any look I want before I even set foot outside the door.

Unfortunately, I've fallen victim in the past to the same vicious cycle I have a feeling might sound all too familiar to you: in the pain of a breakup, my self-confidence would plummet to way below zero; one look in the mirror told me my low self-confidence was perfectly justified, and I couldn't for the life of me find the energy or the motivation to try to do anything about that sad, pale, forlorn reflection gazing pitifully back at me from that cruel mirror. After being told often enough by myself and my heartbreaker that I wasn't worth making a fuss over, what was the point of going to all that trouble anyway?

Finally—call it an occupational hazard or an occupational bonus—I had no choice but to break that cycle. Unless I was auditioning for a role as a homeless insomniac with a puffy eye condition (those roles don't come up too often on soaps), I had to either pull myself together for auditions or risk being evicted. And eviction, I assure you, was *not* going to happen! I'll proudly bus tables at a truck-stop diner before I'll let my bills fall by the wayside.

So I started pulling myself together against my will, and over the course of a week or two I "discovered" something I'm sure I already knew: the reflection we see in the mirror or in those booby traps called store windows has a direct effect on how we feel. There was no doubt about it, the more effort I put into myself the better I looked, the better I looked the better I felt, and the better I felt the more effort I put into myself. It was a great lesson, forced on me by circumstance or not, and I'm excited for this opportunity to share it with you because it made such a big difference in such a relatively short time.

Feeling sad and anxious? Primp and pamper yourself. Feeling that you're not really worth the trouble? Primp and pamper yourself even more, because your worth is incalculable and it's time you experience that fact once and for all. And I'll tell you something else about investing time in our God-given right to be gorgeous: there are a lot of things in life we can't control, and those can be hard to deal with, especially when one of them is a broken heart. But we *can* control how we look and feel when we walk out the door, and it's time to get started.

I love cosmetics. In fact, before I was an actress, I was a professional makeup artist. When my soap opera career was well under way, I started expressing my strong opinions about the best and worst of the cosmetics on the market in my own monthly *Soap Opera Digest* column called "Product Queen." And finally, frustrated by everything from the price to the quality to the selection of makeup out there, I started meeting with chemists and creating my version of "doing it right." My company is called Cat Cosmetics, and it was born in my *One Life to Live* dressing room. (Yet another thing I was told by countless people I simply couldn't do, and eight years later it's still going strong. Come visit at www.catcosmetics.com.)

All of which is to explain my need to grab you by the hand and pull you excitedly to your makeup mirror to show you how easily you can elevate and even reinvent yourself with the right products, a little guidance, and very little effort and *definitely* without breaking the bank. No need to qualify these tips and recommendations based on your age either. I literally growl when I see magazines devote pages and pages to what cosmetics you should wear when you're in your twenties, thirties, forties, fifties, or sixties. Who says? No wonder we women feel insecure about getting older when it's made into such an issue for no good reason. How about celebrating the wisdom and beauty we earn and exude *because* we're getting older? The truth is, we get better every year, and it's up to us to know it and show it.

I say, wear what makes you happy and what makes you feel good. Period. It doesn't need to be any more complicated than that. So here are my suggestions for an ideal beauty arsenal, whether you're twenty-one or sixty-eight:

- A bronzer you love
- A lipstick or lip gloss you love
- An eyeliner you love (pencil, liquid, or gel, whatever you prefer)
- A mascara you love (skip department stores and head straight to the drugstore)
- An excellent quality bronzer brush

That's it. Those are the only basics you need. The zillion or so additional products available on the market are lots of fun, but purely optional.

The essential components of skin care are every bit as basic and affordable, and make no mistake about it, skin care is as important as makeup, if not more so. Some of you prefer not to wear makeup at all, and you at your most beautiful starts with your preferences and your enhanced self-confidence. Cosmetics can only gild the lily, and the lily is your soft, supple, clean, exfoliated, and moisturized skin. The cleanser, exfoliator, and moisturizer you choose (along with an eye cream if you like) don't need to be expensive. In fact, I'm going to pass along a secret that the creator of a very expensive line of skin products once whispered to a friend of mine (and you'll never get the name out of me): "My products are good, but just between us, they're no better than most of the brands you can find in any drugstore at a fraction of the price." Enough said? It's not the price or the prestige of the label, it's the reliable daily routine of cleansing, exfoliating, and moisturizing that makes all the difference.

So. First thing every morning, a nice hot shower, which will take care of the "puffies."

Then the skin care, to create a refreshed, beautiful canvas—the work of art that you are.

Then, if you choose, what I call my "cup of coffee for the face," three to five minutes that will send you out the door with a little extra spring in your step, because it proves that no one deserves three to five minutes of your time more than you do:

1. Take your nice, soft, dense, fat bronzer brush and *lightly* dust your entire face with your bronzer (preferably brown-and-gold-based, rather than red- or orange-based, by the way). Put a little extra effort onto the cheekbones, and always brush *up* when applying color. *Up* is your friend. It gives a subtle lifting effect that brightens the face.

2. Line the eyes, as close to the lashes as you can possibly get, being careful not to make the line too thick—that "Sharpie" look can create a harsh, brittle effect. Now smudge the liner *into* the lashes with a small brush or Q-tip so that it looks like part of the eye, as if you were born that way. Make the upper and lower outer corners of the eye a little darker, to make the eyes "pop." And don't worry about making it perfect. This is an unstructured and very natural look when you're through.

3. Apply one to two coats of mascara.

Now, it's time for your lipstick or lip gloss. If you want to take a few years off your face, bear in mind that darker shades, particularly purple-based ones, are notorious at making us look older. Earthy gold, pink, and brown shades are safe, beautiful, and natural, and if you prefer red, just remember that the red-brown shades are often more flattering than the red-blue shades.

The end! Your cup of coffee for the face, in less than five minutes—or it will be with just a day or two of practice.

Want to add foundation or concealer to the routine? I find that most women really need very little, if any. But if you prefer to wear them—and again, this is all about *you*—apply them first, then proceed with the four previous steps. Think of it as preparing the canvas to accept the colors of your artwork.

If you're a lip liner girl, just remember that lip liners aren't supposed to reinvent the lips, they're just meant to enhance them. Use a nude-colored liner and avoid drawing outside the lip line. A pale gold gloss happens to be lovely over almost any color, by the way, and even looks great with just a lip liner underneath.

There. Thank you so much for indulging me on one of my favorite subjects, and please know that my only intention with all this enthusiasm was and is to make it sound like fun, rather than work, to get you back out there looking and feeling every bit as spectacular as you are.

And don't you ever again let anyone, not even you, try to tell you that you're not worth the effort!

Today's Affirmation

I am a beautiful woman, which I honor every day by making myself look as good as I want to feel. My daily routine reflects the fact that I love who I am and how I look, and I'm proud to show the world that my outer beauty is only a mirror image of the beauty I carry inside.

DAY 28

Resources for
Future Reference

Knowledge is power.

—Sir Francis Bacon

I obviously hope you've learned some things in this time we've spent together that you didn't know before, or that maybe you'd lost track of in this tough time you're putting behind you. More than anything else, though, I hope you've learned this: you are an utterly unique, fascinating work in progress, worth every bit of time and energy and love you can possibly invest, with your greatest potential still ahead of you, no matter what your age or how firmly convinced you were just a few short weeks ago that your life has already been as good as it gets.

I'm a voracious reader and an avid web surfer. I can safely say I've made my way through some of the most invaluable, and some of the most worthless, books and websites available in pursuit of my own self-knowledge and in preparation for writing this book. It would make me so happy if you'd keep right on devoting some time to your growth, your exploration of yourself and your dreams every single day after our thirty days together is over. With that hope in mind, I've put together a few "recommended reading" lists on a handful of the subjects we've talked about so that you can keep right on researching anything and everything that intrigued you along the way.

Your only exercise for today: take out your journal/diary/workbook and make your own reading list from these suggestions. Then I want you to buy or get from the library at least one of the books on your list so that it's there for you to look forward to on Day 31, to insure that you won't lose this amazing momentum you've achieved.

In Case You Don't Already Know ...

www.amazon.com: Amazon is a favorite of mine because you can buy new *and* used books, and shipping is fast and reliable.

Personal Growth

You Can Heal Your Life by Louise L. Hay
The Language of Letting Go by Melody Beattie
Co-Dependent No More by Melody Beattie
Self Matters by Dr. Philip McGraw
Women and Money by Suze Orman

The Gift of Fear by Gavin De Becker
Life Strategies by Dr. Philip McGraw
www.womenwholaunch.com
www.suzeorman.com
www.oprah.com
www.alancohen.com
www.thelearningannex.org

Relationships

Attracting Terrific People by Lillian Glass
He's Just Not That into You by Greg Behrendt and Liz Tuccillo
Emotional Vampires by Albert Bernstein
Walking on Eggshells by Paul T. Mason and Randy Kreger
Men Are from Mars, Women Are from Venus by John Gray

Weight Management

Fast and Easy by Suzanne Somers
Fit for Life by Harvey Diamond and Marilyn Diamond
The Ultimate Weight Solution: The 7 Keys to Weight Loss Freedom by Dr. Philip McGraw
The Best Life Diet by Bob Greene
www.weightwatchers.com
www.weightview.com
www.suzannesomers.com
www.jennycraig.com
www.nutrisystem.com

Spiritual Growth

The Power of Now by Eckhart Tolle
A New Earth by Eckhart Tolle
Your Best Life Now by Joel Osteen
Become a Better You by Joel Osteen
A Deep Breath of Life by Alan Cohen
The Law of Attraction by Esther and Jerry Hicks
The Secret by Rhonda Byrne
*The Other Side and Back: A Psychic's Guide to Our World and
  Beyond* by Sylvia Browne and Lindsay Harrison
Think and Grow Rich by Napoleon Hill
Living Loving and Learning by Leo Buscaglia
A Course in Miracles by Marianne Williamson
www.eckharttolle.com
www.thesecret.tv

Beauty

The Black Book of Hollywood Beauty Secrets by Kym Douglas
  and Cindy Pearlman
Making Faces by Kevyn Aucoin
www.catcosmetics.com
www.drugstore.com
www.sephora.com
www.megsmakeup.com
www.makeupalley.com

Today's Affirmation

I hereby make this joyful commitment to myself: that the day I stop learning will be the day I stop living.

DAY 29

The Great Life

We are not human beings having a spiritual experience. We are spiritual beings having a human experience.

—TEILHARD DE CHARDIN

You're almost there. It's graduation eve. I'm excited for you, and I admire you so much for the hard work and discipline it's taken to reach this day, especially when I know there were days when just getting out of bed was a challenge. You haven't just survived your heartbreak—you've *won*. You're amazing, and your life will just keep getting better and better from this day on; you'll see to that.

I hope this book will continue to be a source of support and friendship, that you'll revisit particular lessons, exercises, or affirmations that intrigued or challenged you. I also hope you've adopted a few new healthy, positive mental and emotional habits based on what we've worked on together, habits that will give you more strength or insight or clarity or joy or peace of mind that you had before we met.

Twenty-eight days' worth of material is a lot to remember as you move ahead with your busy, exciting life. So to make it easier, I just want to summarize by giving you the five basic steps to the true art of human *being* to carry in your heart from now on:

1. Shake Off the Past

Don't get me wrong; the past has some value. It's the source of our most hard-won wisdom and lessons, and it's where our treasured memories live.

But it's also where our pain bubble lurks, that space we can easily fall into where we're overwhelmed by our wounds while the rest of the world waits for us to come back to the present tense, get over ourselves, and join the party. There's not one thing to be gained from revisiting that pain bubble. We hurt quite enough when those wounds were inflicted, don't you think? When have we ever helped a wound to heal by continuing to open it and refusing to leave it alone?

You've done the past already. You don't have to do it again. Besides, the more time you spend back there, the more you're missing out on right here, and right now, and right here, and right now is where life is, where you can make all the positive changes you want, where you can make a difference. Right here, and right now is the only reality you need to concern yourself with. Right here, and right now all that drama and fear are gone. You're safe and you're fine, *right here, and right now*, spending your precious time with me, and you know by now that I won't abuse the privilege.

You're not a robot. You're bound to slip back into thinking about your heartbreaker from time to time, and you're allowed—on condition that you focus on all the useful lessons you learned, either because of or in spite of him, and the happy fact that he's no longer your problem. The minute thinking about him starts to stir up negativity, pain, sadness, or anxiety in you, those thoughts have outlived their usefulness, they're only to your detriment, and they can accomplish nothing more than feeding your old, outdated habit of being unhappy and unsettled.

From now on, whenever you mentally start down a path into the past that's not either a happy memory or a worthwhile lesson learned, I want you to picture a battalion of gatekeepers forming an impenetrable line of protection at the entrance to your mind. Actually hear them yell in unison, a firm, "Halt!" That quick conscious alarm will be your cue to change those thoughts one thought at a time, from the negative past to something comforting about right here, and right now, even if it's as trivial as, "I'm perfectly calm and peaceful, minding my own business, reading this book, and working on myself, and nobody gets to interrupt."

From now on, order those gatekeepers to let nothing but positive thoughts into your mind. It's not called "the power of positive thinking" for nothing. Positive thoughts create balance and focus and lead to positive action, as you'll discover more and more with each new day ahead.

This is step 1 to the great life, the art of human *being*.

2. Embrace a New Beginning

We all have a certain fondness for the familiar, even when the familiar isn't pretty. "Better the devil we know than the devil we don't know" lies at the core of far too many of our actions and inactions, since any devil at all is unacceptable. I much prefer something a friend of mine says on the subject of refusing to move forward for fear of what might be lurking out there: "Standing still is only a good idea if you happen to be standing in a good place."

It's especially important to loosen our grip on the familiar when what's familiar is loss and grief. And you already made the choice to reject that particular familiarity the day you opened this book. You're my hero for choosing to pursue thirty days of joy, wisdom, and healing, rather than resigning yourself to months, or even years, of hoping all that hurt would just go away because you didn't know what else to do about it. You stepped up for yourself and said, "Enough is enough. I don't want to feel this way anymore. I have the power to choose, and I choose to be free from this darkness and receive my right to joy."

The operative words in that sentence are "free" and "joy." You *are* free, and joy is all around you, waiting to be discovered. You're available to fall in love with yourself, and with your life, whatever you want it to look like, wherever you want it to happen, and whoever deserves, by virtue of their own pursuit of joy, to share it with you. When you fall in love with your life, it's amazing, and reliable, that your life falls in love with you right back, and it's a love that keeps right on growing if you simply continue nourishing it with the sense of newness, curiosity, willingness, and delight every new day deserves.

Be excited by the fact that your life is a portrait of the choices you've made, and your future will be a portrait of the healthier, wiser, more responsible choices that lie ahead. *You* get to choose. The power is yours, and you're learning to use it well. Celebrate that as you stride into your gorgeous new adventures. Come to think of it, celebrate *everything*.

3. Have Fun

Grief is a dark, cramped, suffocating place. Thank God you're not there anymore, because there's just no fun to be had there. And guess what? A fair percentage of the time, *life is supposed to be fun*! That's not just a theoretical fact, it's a physiological one. Laughter releases endorphins, and endorphins have been proven to reduce pain, lower blood pressure, and even create sensations of euphoria. So don't just sit there—start having fun!

It's not for me to dictate what's fun for you. I know that fun for me ranges from a quick daily trip to Youtube.com for some laughs that reach all the way to my knees, to getting together with friends one night a week for a potluck dinner and a particular TV show we're addicted to, to some serious romping with my beloved dogs, to meeting some pals for a night of silly games as corny as Win, Lose, or Draw or the perpetually entertaining Trivial Pursuit, to just me and my animals cuddled up in bed with a bowl of popcorn watching a favorite movie. Whatever works for you, have at it, with one strong suggestion: please be sure to schedule at least one fun event for yourself each and every week, as surely and diligently as you make time for your job and all your other responsibilities. You need it, you deserve it, you can use the endorphins, and it's a crucial element of a life not just endured but thoroughly enjoyed. A great life, in fact.

4. Get Your Fire Back

You went through a heartbreak, and chances are the heart-breaker was the undeserving repository of a lot of your passion and a lot of your dreams. I can't stress this enough: he wasn't the *source* of them! He didn't take them away with him! He may be gone, but your passion and your dreams are still yours, safe, worthwhile, and perfectly intact. They just need to be rewritten, redirected, and reignited.

Light a fire under the dreams you'd forgotten until now. Light a fire under the dreams you put off or extinguished for your heartbreaker's convenience. Dream new dreams and light a fire under those too. They all have the potential to take you to brand-new exciting places and people, and no one can take them away from you unless you let it happen. If someone tells you a dream is beyond your reach, use me as your poster child. I wish I had a dollar for every time someone told me I wasn't good enough, or pretty enough, or old enough, or young enough. And so what? Who says? Nine times out of ten I just went out and made my dreams come true anyway. That tenth time out of ten, that dream that refused to be realized? Again, and so what? I just dreamed a new one and lit a fire under that.

It's time to dream those dreams again, and light those flames of passion to propel them into reality. Because it's only the most passionate, hardworking, determined dreamers who truly understand the art of human being.

5. Get Grateful

Did you know that it's impossible to be angry and grateful at the same time? Or frightened and grateful? Or depressed and grateful?

If that doesn't motivate us to stay in a state of gratitude as often as possible, I can't imagine what will, because I hate being angry, frightened, and depressed.

Sometimes gratitude is hard to achieve, I know. Our lives aren't always a nonstop game of hopscotch in a leafy glade, nor should they be—there's not a lot of learning and growth potential in a lifetime of hopscotch. And anything we learn and grow from deserves our gratitude, which means it wasn't a mistake, which means that, just for starters in our search for gratitude, we can redefine and thank ourselves for any number of things we might still be privately kicking ourselves for.

The point is, while some gratitude-inspiring moments and events make themselves obvious, most of them are hiding quietly right under our noses, waiting for us to acknowledge them:

- Every new, as yet unwritten, day
- That first bite of food when you're truly hungry
- The feel of your body sinking onto your bed when you're exhausted
- The security of having a job
- The sound of a friend's voice
- Your favorite TV show, especially when you're watching in your jammies
- Your car starting just like it's supposed to
- Having a whole year to go before your next mammogram
- A book you just can't put down
- Your animals
- A hot bubble bath
- Freshly laundered sheets
- A movie that makes you laugh, or cry, every time you watch it

You get the idea. It's worth stopping for a moment to recognize and express your gratitude for even the tiniest thing that you may have been taking for granted until now—out loud. If you think I'm exaggerating any of my friends and co-workers will back me up on this: I make gratitude announcements several times a day, no matter where I am or who, if anyone, is around. I'll stop whatever I'm doing for a quick, "I just want to take a moment to say that I am feeling *so* grateful right now." My coworkers don't mind a bit, my friends are used to it, people even seem to get a kick out of it. And even if they didn't, I'd keep right on doing it, because I find that I'm having more and more gratitude moments simply because I honor them.

There is no such thing as a great life without gratitude, so remember to say thank you—out loud, often, and from your heart—as you create your own world of joy.

Today's Affirmation

My great life is waiting for me, and I am ready to receive it. Life is precious. People are precious. I am precious. I am so eager to share all the fun and kindness and love and healing and gratitude that have come alive again inside me as I let go of the past once and for all, and create a new ending by embracing a new beginning.

DAY 30

Graduation Day

Pray as if all depends on God, and act as if all depends on you.

—GEORGE WASHINGTON CARVER

Congratulations, my treasured soul, for making it through these past thirty days and doing it with such faith and commitment. Reaching this day means you chose to heal, to invest in and celebrate your whole, smart, beautiful self, to work through your heartbreak and fall in love with *yourself*, either again or for the first time in your life. It took courage to walk this path, and you stepped up to the plate. You've learned and grown so much from what you've been through, and I am *so* proud of you. Life will always be filled with twists and turns, but you'll handle the curves with so much more wisdom and perspective from now on, thanks to your insistence on a life of health and happiness instead of the pain you couldn't see past just one short—and sometimes endless—month ago.

The old saying that time heals everything is a myth. Time

by itself heals nothing at all. It's how you use that time that matters, and you've made this time matter. You're already seeing with your own eyes that "a bend in the road is not the end of the road," that very often a bend in the road is the universe's way of offering us the choice of a brand-new start. And beyond this bend in the road you'll discover, as you need them, the answers to why you went through all this. In fact, if you keep using the skills you learned or relearned in the past thirty days and remember to never, ever lose the lessons, mark my words, the day will come when you'll say, "If that's what it took to get me where I am now, I'd do it again."

As I release you to live your healthiest, happiest, most beautiful dreams, I want to remind you one more time that the most important relationship we'll ever have is our relationship with ourselves! After all, we're the experts when it comes to us. So why should we expect anyone else to enjoy our company if we don't? How can we expect anyone else to cherish and honor us if we make it clear that we don't cherish and honor ourselves? Don't spend one moment of one day from this day forward settling for less than the best of the best, from you or from anyone else.

Never again think of life as all those things that happen to us between the time we live and the time we die. Once we've grown past childhood, life at any given moment is the sum total of the choices we make, and we are responsible for those choices. Choose wisely. Choose anything and everything that will lead you closer to your highest potential as a daughter, sister, friend, employee, wife, girlfriend, mother, and whatever other roles you choose to tackle. Choose anything and every-thing that will simplify, complement, and enhance your life, leaving the others to their chaos and turmoil. Choose san-ity. Choose peace. Choose serenity. Choose kindness. Choose freedom, in the many forms it takes.

Just think, from this moment on, your life is yours to cre-ate. What a thrilling time this is now that you have the skills, tools, and wisdom to make it soar. I'm excited for you, and from the bottom of my heart, I believe in you.

Today's Exercises

First, a few loose ends to tie up.

I want you to call, write notes, or e-mail those people who've been there for you in these past rough thirty days. Tell them how much their friendship and patience helped get you to this wonderful place you are now, and promise (and mean it) that you'll do exactly the same for them if and when they ever need you.

I want you to plan a great celebration dinner for yourself. And since it's your celebration, you choose the agenda—a nice restaurant, a home-cooked meal, a potluck picnic at the park, just make it as special and joyful as you are.

Last but not least, I want you to turn to your calendar and make sure there's a nice big *X* through every single one of those thirty days. You've more than earned every one of them. Then, when you've finished these next few paragraphs, I want you to take this book and your journal/diary/workbook and put them in a very special place for future reference. You may not even understand yet how far you've come, but just you wait until you get them back out again a few months from now. Your jaw will hit the floor.

There. Now, I want you to make yourself very comfortable and, after reading the rest of this last exercise, take three deep breaths and close your eyes, so that you can really *see* this with me.

I want you to put an actual form, a body, an image to the pain you felt from this heartbreak. The pain can look like your heartbreaker, or a spider, or your old chemistry teacher. It really doesn't matter, just make it easy for you to visualize.

Now, you're going to put that image of your pain inside a clear giant helium balloon, floating directly above you. There's a rope tied to that huge balloon, and you're gripping that rope with both hands to keep the balloon from floating away.

Your arms are straight up in the air and your hands are tightened around the thick rough rope, straining against the incredible heaviness of the pain inside that balloon that's pulling it up and away from you. It's so strong, and it weighs so much, that you have to struggle to keep it from pulling you off the ground. More than once you almost lose your balance and your footing. Your arms are getting so tired, and the rope is chafing against the palms of your hands.

Suddenly, your hold gives way and you release the rope. You watch, helpless, as the balloon floats up into the blue sky. You even jump up and reach to grab the rope again until you see the image of your pain inside the balloon. Then, with a long exhale, you stop reaching and just let it go. The sun glints off the sparkling clear balloon as you stand motionless, watching the balloon become smaller and smaller, taking your pain with it, and before long it's completely disappeared . . . from your sight, from your mind, from your heart.

You find yourself smiling, a smile so deep and so long overdue that it reaches all the way to your soul. You feel light as a feather, free from pain, free from anger, free from grief, and yet there's great comfort in feeling how firmly and safely your feet are planted on solid ground.

Your eyes fill with tears of gratitude for all you've learned and for the amazing life those lessons are about to make possible. You've never been more capable of loving, and because of that, you know you've never been more capable of being loved.

You take one more look into the sky. There's no sign of your pain. There's nothing up there but the sun, shining on your beautiful face.

You can't wait to show the world the best of yourself.

You can't wait to experience your power, your importance, your generosity, and how very much you matter.

Your best life is just beginning.

Your peace, your joy, and your love are on their way.

Now, open your eyes, give yourself a long tight loving hug from me along with my gratitude for letting me share this time with you, and go have an amazing life!